Great Theme Parties for Children

Compiled by Irene N. Watts

♫ Sterling Publishing Co., Inc.   New York

For Julia

Library of Congress Cataloging-in-Publication Data

Watts, Irene N.
    Great theme parties for children / Irene N. Watts.
       p.   cm.
    Includes index.
    Summary: Plans for giving eleven theme parties, including
Halloween, winter, animals, and detectives, with suggestions for
invitations, food, games, videos, and read-aloud books.
    ISBN 0-8069-7410-9
    1. Children's parties—Juvenile literature. 2. Games—Juvenile
literature. [1. Parties.] I. Title.
GV1205.W38   1991
793.2'1—dc20
                                     90-47067
                                       CIP
                                       AC

10 9 8 7 6 5 4 3 2 1

© 1991 by Irene N. Watts
Published by Sterling Publishing Company, Inc.
387 Park Avenue South, New York, N.Y. 10016
This is an expanded edition of *The Great Detective Party
and Other Theme Games for Children* originally published by
Pembroke Publishers Ltd, Ontario
Distributed in Great Britain and Europe by Cassell PLC
Villiers House, 41/47 Strand, London WC2N 5JE, England
Distributed in Australia by Capricorn Ltd.
P.O. Box 665, Lane Cove, NSW 2066
Manufactured in the United States of America
All rights reserved

Sterling ISBN 0-8069-7410-9 Trade

Contents

Before You Begin

Some years ago I was invited to give drama workshops at the Fort Chipewayan Indian School in northern Alberta, Canada. At the end of the day I joined the Girls' Residence attached to the school for supper. After the tables had been cleared, thirty little girls aged six to twelve looked at me expectantly. I produced a balloon, and a thick felt pen, and we sat on the floor in a circle as I explained the rules. Everyone would have a turn in drawing on the balloon but the moment the tip of the pen left the surface of the balloon the turn was over. Of course, we discussed at length the fact that we had to be very, very gentle, or the balloon would burst. It took over thirty minutes to get round that circle, and the breathless anticipation (and tension, would the balloon burst?) of waiting for one's turn didn't seem long at all. Finally we had our "balloon picture"—a face—and the suggestions for the story came quickly. It became the beginning of a family, and we had to create several more family members.

Since then, I have played that game and many other games with children from reservations across Alberta and from the remotest regions of the Northwest Territories, in kindergartens, elementary and high schools and private homes in Nova Scotia, Ontario, British Columbia, the United Kingdom, and West Germany. We have played traditional games, and made up new ones and created stories. The stimulus has always been a particular theme: whether a birthday party with a pirate motif, a Halloween party, or a creative writing class about the circus, we have chosen games within the framework of that theme.

I began playing and teaching when my own four children were small. Now I work with their children and with other people's, discovering new games and fresher ways to present and play the traditional and familiar. I've learned some tips to help me along the way, and I hope they will also be useful to those of you starting out.

Special occasions may be as formal as the birthday or Valentines' party with planned games, prizes, and food, or they can be as spontaneous as a game or story to summarize an activity, a unit of work, or just to end the day. This book is for all those occasions. There are many choices.

You may be looking for a full day's event to fit in with a sports day, then *The Great Outdoors* or *Wild West* provide enough material. However, this is not a recipe book to be followed exactly; instead I hope you will dip in and find a game that suits your theme, for you will discover that many ideas with just the smallest change will suit several themes. The read-aloud books, too, are a very personal choice, being really just a starting point, and you may have a much more suitable choice for your particular group and occasion. In the same way that the games can be adapted and used in different themes, so the stories often lend themselves to more than one occasion. *Morgan the Magnificent*, by Ian Wallace, is about a little girl who wants to join the circus; obviously, this may be read both for *Clown* and *I Want to Be*.

These are only my suggestions for you to build on. The most rewarding themes, of course, will be the ones you discover for yourself.

1. Preparation

It's really worthwhile to have all the items needed for each activity ready well in advance and in one easy-to-find place. This avoids restlessness by eliminating long waits between games.

2. Introductions

Do make sure that everyone knows everyone by name, including "helpers" and, if you are having a party in an unfamiliar setting, the whereabouts of the bathroom.

3. Games, Pacing and Structure

Explain each game, slowly and carefully, and where applicable have a trial round. No one likes being "out" the first time. However, keep the pace of the game fairly fast moving. It's preferable to change a game while the guests are still having fun, than to risk going on until they are bored. For example, a tag game played three times is probably ample.

4. Contrasts

Alternate fast moving games with quiet ones. This has been allowed for in the themes, but if you select only a few games from a particular theme, do make sure that they do not all require the same kind of energy.

5. Flexibility

The length of the activities will vary according to the age, interest and stamina of the group. *YOU* don't have to do it all! Be ready to switch your planned order, moving on to something quieter or to something more energetic if the mood of the group is not in tune with what you have prepared.

6. Invitations

Be specific about when the party begins and ends; state clearly if children should be in costume, or need to bring anything.

7. Opening and Closing Activities

Waiting for all the guests to arrive, so that the party can get going, is always difficult. Because of this, every single theme opens with a "warmup" that may begin with the first arrivals, but which late-comers can join easily. Suggestions for reading aloud and/or watching video movies are optional; they have been included primarily for sleepover parties, or school and community groups where there are large numbers gathered for a longer period of time. I have found that closing the party with reading aloud from a book that reflects the theme of the celebration is a meaningful "drawing together" at the end.

8. Space

If your home is small, there are many solutions: Cut down numbers to four, five or six. Remove as much furniture from the party space as possible—most children prefer sitting on the floor, anyway. Whatever the size of the space, this, plus removing breakables, is a good solution. A possible option might be to borrow your local park, church or community hall basement, or even the school gym.

9. Agreed Signals

For larger groups, particularly outdoors, agree on a signal that will bring everyone immediately to a stop and/or to gather round to hear the next instruction. A plastic slide whistle is ideal, but really any sound that carries will do. Agree, and then have a trial run.

10. Costumes/Hats

Raid your own and your friends' closets; your local theatre group may be able to help you also.

11. Size of Group

My own ideal is one adult for every eight children (six if the children are preschool). If the group is over 20, I would advise three adults or teens. The game explanations can be shared between you, and of course everyone joins in.

12. Children as Hosts and Organizers

Children love planning a celebration for others. A Grade Five class might be ready to have a party for the Grade One or Kindergarten group.

The students can team up to explain and run the games, to read the final story, to buy and prepare the food.

A welcome party for a new class member, or someone new to the neighborhood, especially if from another country, would be an ideal opportunity to make friends.

Finally *do* use your creativity to adapt, add, omit and transpose games from theme to theme. Enjoy yourselves!

The Great Detective Party

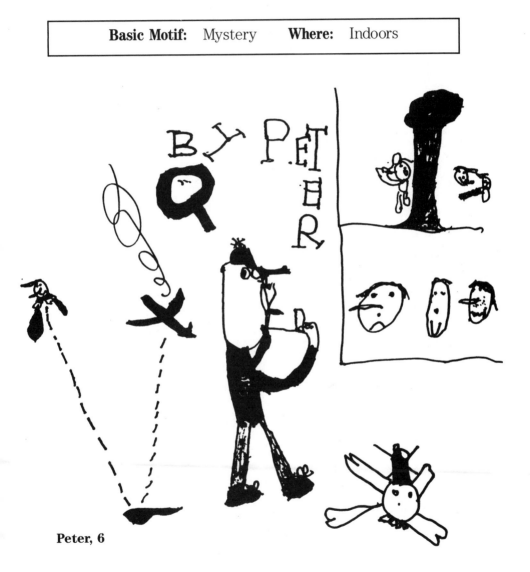

Peter, 6

TO DETECT: To discover, uncover, notice, observe, see, spot, investigate, catch ...

1. STOLEN MONEY

Number of Players:	4–Unlimited
Age Range:	7–Adult
Preparation:	Pennies and nickels, at least two per guest
	Name tags designed in the form of a Sheriff's badge
	Each child's name is printed on the tag.

Pennies have been hidden carefully all over the play area. As guests arrive, they are handed their badges with their full names printed on them. The object of the game is to locate as many of the hidden coins as possible—but *not* to pick them up. The players are simply supposed to remember exactly where they are. It is also important to remember to keep the coins' location a secret from the other people who may be looking for them.

Once all the guests have arrived and have had a few minutes to find some coins, divide them into two teams. Each team pools its information. After that, they compare their findings to see which side has the most accurate information. Then the coins are retrieved for the next game.

In a variation, this game can be an individual contest, with the two most successful "Detectives" becoming the team leaders for the next game.

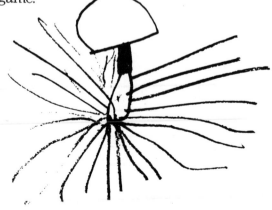

Taylor, 9

2. HIDDEN LOOT

Number of Players:	4–Unlimited
Age Range:	6–Adult
Preparation:	A supply of small coins—about 50 cents worth

The two teams from "Stolen Money" are given the title of the "Bank Robbers" and "The Detectives." Or if you've played that game as an individual contest, have the two "winners" from the previous game choose sides.

The Detective team leaves the room for a couple of minutes. During this time, the Bank Robbers hide their loot (coins). When the Detectives are recalled, they are given three minutes to find the "stolen money." They collect the coins and count up how much of the original sum they have recovered. Next the situation is reversed. This time the Detectives conceal the coins from the Bank Robbers. Exactly the same conditions apply. Which team will win?

3. STEAL THE TREASURE

Number of Players:	4–Unlimited
Age Range:	6–Adult
Preparation:	A chair
	A blindfold
	Coins or small objects such as marbles, shells, pencils, etc.

A member of the "winning team" from "Hidden Loot" is blindfolded and, in the role of "The Great Detective," sits in a chair. Coins are scattered around his feet, and it is his duty to guard them in the night. One or two thieves (depending on the size of the group) at a time attempt to steal the money, but if The Great Detective hears their approach, and can point to any of them accurately, they are "jailed" and out of the game. The game is usually played several times with a different Detective on guard.

The competition is to see which detective can apprehend the most prisoners. It is also a game of skill and competition between "thieves" and "detectives."

A slightly different version, played without a blindfold, works well in a smaller area. You can play it simultaneously with two groups. The Detective sits on the floor surrounded by coins or objects. The Thieves sit around him. Neither Thieves nor Detectives must move from their places. However, the Thieves must distract the Detective in any way (other than physically) so that they may steal one of the coins. If a coin can be removed and put behind the Thief while the Detective is not looking, it is considered a "successful theft." Three minute time limit for each Detective.

Spies

Taylor, 9

4. FIND THE BOMB

Number of Players:	4–Unlimited
Age Range:	7–Adult
Preparation:	An alarm clock with a loud tick, concealed very carefully in the party room

The guests, who have been waiting outside, are told they only have a short time before a bomb is set to go off, and that the bomb is hidden in the party room. It is set to go off, say, five minutes before the hour. Whoever finds it must stop the alarm before it rings. This makes for incredible suspense, of course! If the clock is not found, the alarm will ring and the entire group is "blown up."

For a slightly longer game, guests can work in pairs to locate the bomb and it can be hidden afresh for each team.

In either case, you need to time the game very carefully. Allow the searchers about five minutes to find the "bomb."

5. WHO ARE YOU?

Number of Players:	4–25
Age Range:	6–Adult
Preparation:	A blindfold

This is another game that builds concentration. In order for it to work properly, the children first must listen to each other's voices. All sit in a circle and take turns speaking the following line: "My name is Detective Inspector John (or Mary)", depending on their real names. When everyone has had a turn, one child goes into the middle of the circle and becomes the Detective, while all the others are criminals. The Detective is blindfolded, turned around several times. Then he or she points to any "criminal" and asks "Who are you?"

The object of the game is for the players to disguise their identities, by changing their true voices, and giving false names. Instead of saying "I'm Detective Inspector Mary," for example, the answer might be "I'm the tax collector," or "I'm the window cleaner."

Each Detective is allowed two guesses, unless the group is very small, in which case only one guess is allowed. If the Detective correctly identifies the criminal, another Detective takes his place.

6. SILENT WITNESS

Number of Players:	6–Unlimited
Age Range:	7–Adult
Preparation:	None

Children remain standing or seated, and are given 30 seconds to observe each other in silence. They are told that this is their last chance to observe the "witnesses." The players then turn away and change two things in their appearance. A shoelace may be undone, a button may be opened, a cuff turned. A child is chosen to be the Detective. He or she now attempts to name as many of the changes as possible. Repeat the game with different Detectives.

A variation of the game is for only three people in the lineup to change their appearance. The Detective must guess who the three are, as well as the changes they have made. If the group is very large, you can play this game simultaneously with two teams, or with one team watching until it is their turn.

7. A CRIME HAS BEEN COMMITTED

Number of Players:	6–Unlimited
Age Range:	9–Adult
Preparation:	A large sheet of paper that covers an entire table
	A large cloth
	Five or six objects, such as

a motel or house key

an airline, bus or train ticket

a theatre ticket stub

an envelope with an unusual address or name on it, preferably with a foreign stamp

a small dictionary in another language

a box of matches from a restaurant or nightclub

a left-handed glove

an empty pill box

a silk scarf, etc.

Pencils and notepads for each team

Two prizes for the winning team

Place six objects on paper on a table. Outline each object with chalk or felt pen, so that if it is moved you can place it back in its original position exactly. Cover the objects with a cloth until the start of the game.

In this game everyone is a Detective. Everyone works with a partner, and each team is given a pad and pencil to make notes. They are then asked to solve a crime, and are given the following information, before they have the opportunity to examine the clues: "These objects have been recovered from the scene of a crime." (Depending on the objects, this may be a house, a hotel room, an apartment, train or restaurant.) "No actual body has been discovered yet, but someone is missing."

The teams must answer the following questions as well as make a decision about the dead or missing persons.

1. Who committed the crime?
2. What is the nature of the crime? (for instance, blackmail, kidnapping, espionage, etc.)
3. Why did it happen?
4. When did it occur?
5. Over how long a period of time?
6. Where did it take place? Was more than one location involved?
7. Who is the victim, or is there more than one?

All clues must be accounted for by logical explanations that are linked in a plausible way. Teams take turns giving their explanations. Allow at least ten minutes, longer is better. A prize is given for the most interesting and ingenious solution.

Obviously, there is no "correct" solution to this investigation—any six objects will do. However, the person who designs the clues must be able to come up with some kind of story that will use all the objects, in case the guests cannot.

8. I CAUGHT A THIEF, HE WAS DOING THIS . . .

Number of Players:	4–Unlimited
Age Range:	8–Adult
Preparation:	None

The guests are told that in their role as detectives they have been tailing an imaginary subject. Each detective imagines the kind of action their "criminal" may have been involved in—smashing a store window, stealing a car, hiding behind a newspaper on a bus or subway, handing over a suspicious parcel to a friend, picking a lock. Each detective in turn, mimes the actions of his imaginary criminal, while the rest of the group guesses the activity.

9. MYSTERY CODE

Number of Players:	4–Unlimited
Age Range:	8–Adult
Preparation:	Words cut at random from magazines and newspapers

The words are placed in the center of a space on the floor or table. The game may be played individually, in pairs, or in groups. Each person—or team—picks up twelve words at random. They now must form these words into a sentence. At least ten of the twelve words must be used in the sentence, for example:

THE BLACK CAT IS HIDDEN IN THE BIG HOUSE AROUND THE CORNER.

or

WHO SAW ME? I AM READING THE BOOK. MEET IN PARK. NOON.

It may or may not be possible to assemble the words in logical sentences. If it isn't, the team can still win if it is able to explain "the code" that is hidden in the text. "The Black Cat" for instance, could be a gang leader who has been kidnapped and hidden in a "safe house." Give a ten minute time limit.

10. MURDER INVESTIGATION

Number of Players:	6–30
Age Range:	8–Adult
Preparation:	Slips of paper, one for each guest
	One says: ENEMY AGENT. One says: DETECTIVE. The remainder say: GUEST
	Taped or live music
	A room that can be blacked out or darkened
	An adult "helper" or "observer"

The guests are told that they are attending a house party. Everyone draws from the pile of papers that is face down. Players must not show their slips to anyone.

Dim the lights and play music softly as the guests walk around or sit and talk or dance. During this time the person who drew the slip of paper with "DETECTIVE" has been waiting outside the room. The killer (Enemy Agent) touches his victim twice on the shoulder; the victim screams loudly and "dies." On the scream the lights are switched on by the adult observer. The Detective, who rushes into the room as soon as he hears the scream of the victim, tells the guests to stay where they are. The victim lies or sits "dead" until the end of the game.

The Detective asks all kinds of questions, such as:

"Where were you at the time of death?"

"Did you notice anything unusual earlier?"

"How well did you know the victim?" and so on. Everyone lies. But when the Detective asks:

"Are you the killer?" the reply must be truthful.

The Detective may only ask this question once in the game. If he is wrong he has lost, and the Enemy Agent has won.

The game is played several times. Detectives should think up a few questions to ask.

Jason, 8

11. MUG SHOT

Number of Players:	4–Unlimited
Age Range:	7–Adult
Preparation:	From magazines and newspapers cut out closeups of faces (they should be as large as possible) and paste them onto cardboard. Then with a pencil and ruler carefully draw lines dividing the picture into four sections. Cut these out. On the back of each puzzle section mark a letter. For example, a picture of Bill Cosby would have a C on the back of each piece.

Competitors team up with a partner (three can work together too). Each person is given one piece of puzzle to start. The rest of the puzzle pieces are spread out on a table or on the floor. They must now find the remaining three pieces to complete the picture, and they may help their partners, as well. Obviously, a lot of exchanging, as well as finding the missing pieces, will have to go on. To prevent grabbing and pushing, try to spread the puzzles over a large surface. A prize is awarded for the first team to complete both pictures.

12. POISON CANDY

Number of Players:	4–Unlimited
Age Range:	5–12
Preparation:	A paper bag or cup for each child
	An assortment of dried fruits, nuts and candies

A dozen or so small candies (the game works better if there is an assortment), nuts, and raisins or even pieces of fruit are placed on a plate. One child is given a small paper bag, and sent outside while the rest of the group decides which one is the "poison candy." Then they call the child back and he or she begins to pick up the candy, one at a time, keeping each one, until the "poison" candy is touched. This ends the child's turn and another child takes a turn. The suspense is enormous: how many candies will the competitor be allowed to keep before the "untouchable" one is reached? It's quite uncanny how children seem to know intuitively which candy to avoid! This game takes a long time.

To Read Aloud:	*Harriet the Spy* by Louise Fitzhugh *The Mysterious Disappearance of Leon (I Mean Noel)* by Ellen Raskin
Video:	*The Pink Panther*: A Blake Edwards Production with Peter Sellers
Snack Suggestions:	Pitas with mystery fillings (chicken salad, cream cheese and raw vegetables, tuna fish) Chinese fortune cookies Miniature jelly rolls
Invitations:	A thumb print on paper with a drawing of a magnifying glass beside it.

I Want To Be

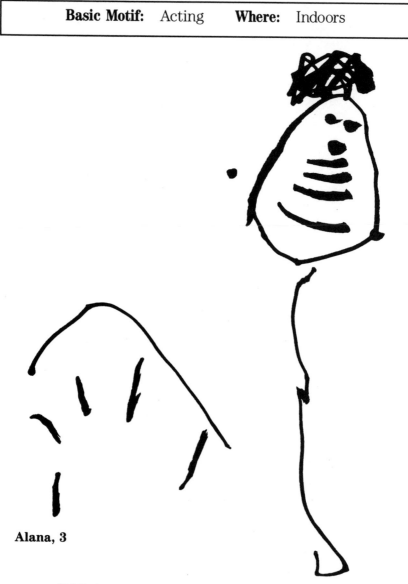

Alana, 3

"*I like acting. I always have, not just watching it but doing it. I like the cheers from the crowd. My name is Becky and I want to be an actress.*"

Becky, 11

1. WHAT AM I DOING?

Number of Players: 2–Unlimited

Age Range: 6–Adult

Preparation: Find a few ordinary household objects, preferably of different shapes and sizes, to encourage all kinds of imaginative ideas, such as:

Wooden spoon

Wastebasket

Comb

Tray

Umbrella or sunshade

Flyswatter

Pencil

Start the game in a place where there will be enough room for all the guests to join the circle as they arrive. The game may begin with as few as two children.

The first person chooses an object and decides on a new way to use it. For example, "I can use this (a comb) as a ..." the child then demonstrates playing the harp. The next person may use the comb as a harmonica; or as a shoe horn; or as corn on the cob. Each activity is mimed, and goes on until the group guesses it correctly.

When all the possibilities of one object have been exhausted (or when the object has gone around the circle once), another one is picked. The game continues until all the guests have arrived and had at least one turn.

If the party is a very large one, the guests can be divided into a couple of groups. Each group is given the same type of objects and the groups then compete to see which one can come up with the most ideas and demonstrate them.

2. SIT BESIDE ME, PLEASE

Number of Players:	4–Unlimited
Age Range:	6–Adult
Preparation:	One chair, cushion or seat per guest plus one extra
	One small sticker per guest

This game requires every child to know left from right. To speed things up, you may want to put a sticker, such as a star, on the back of everyone's right hand; in this way, nobody needs to feel shy about making a mistake!

The chairs are placed in a circle and everyone sits. All the children will know the name of at least one person in the room, so anyone may start. Whoever is sitting to the right of the empty chair begins like this: "I want Jim to sit beside me please." Jim now runs to the empty chair, leaving his original place as the new vacant seat. The person sitting to the right of the vacant seat, must immediately call out another name.

The rules of the game are simple: Move as fast as space permits, and call names clearly and quickly. New ways of moving from chair to chair can be decided on to add to the fun, such as hopping, crawling, walking sideways or backwards. This is a great way to learn everyone's names and to laugh and feel comfortable with each other. Play continues until everyone has had one or two turns.

3. WHEN I GROW UP. . . .

Number of Players:	4–25
Age Range:	8–Adult
Preparation:	None

Start off by forming a circle and asking the children if they know the meaning of the word "mime." Then explain that players will decide on what they'd like to be when they grow up, and give an example, such as typing on an imaginary computer keyboard or writing on an imaginary blackboard. The group guesses the occupation (computer programmer, teacher) and the game can begin.

A volunteer steps into the circle, and says: "I want to be a ..." then mimes the activity. Those watching guess.

In a more complicated version of the game, everyone repeats the sentence and the first mime, and then adds a new one. For instance, Ellen says, "I want to be a traffic cop" and mimes the appropriate actions.

Peter now repeats the phrase, the traffic cop mime, and adds: "I want to be an artist." Then he mimes painting a picture. This continues around the circle. If anyone forgets any part of the sequence, that person is out. In a very large group, the remaining three players could all be designated winners.

4. ACT A HOBBY

Number of Players:	4–30
Age Range:	8–Adult
Preparation:	None

Divide the children into groups of four or five. The groups brainstorm the different leisure activities they like doing. They decide on one hobby that they will perform for the other groups. Five or ten minutes should be enough time to prepare this. Talking is allowed during the performance, as long as the actual *name* of the hobby is not given away during the scene. One group might choose playing in an orchestra, for example. The conductor could count "One, two, three" as he raises his imaginary baton. If the hobby selected is tennis, it would be fine to call out "Good shot," or "Out!". Make sure the audience waits until the scene is completed before guessing the hobby.

5. MIME RELAY RACE

Number of Players:	4–Unlimited
Age Range:	8–Adult
Preparation:	A list of activities (from simple to difficult to perform) printed on separate slips of paper. Examples: SKATEBOARDING, WASHING WINDOWS, TRAINING A PUPPY, TAKING A SHOWER, PLAYING OR SHUFFLING CARDS, JUGGLING THREE BALLS

Choose two guests as team leaders, who take turns selecting their teams. Each team member is then given a number from 1 on. The teams don't have to be even. If one of them has an extra person, that player can take two turns, so that the game is fair. Team members #1 start the game off by going to the leader, who shows them the first activity printed on a slip of paper. If reading presents a problem, the words can be whispered. On a signal "GO," both team members return to their respective teams, and mime the first task. Both teams should be warned not to yell out the answer in their excitement, or they'll give the game away to the opposing team! The person acting out the activity cannot speak in any way, or give any other clues except through making the mime clearer. As soon as the correct answer is given, the #2 person in the team runs to the leader and whispers the correct answer. The leader then reveals the next activity to the #2 player, who runs back to the team and acts it out.

The first team to act and guess all the tasks and stand in the *correct* numerical order, is the winner. This game is usually enjoyed so much—and is often such a close contest—that everyone demands a second round. Other activities that have proved popular are:

EATING AN ICE CREAM CONE, LIGHTING A CAMPFIRE, ROASTING A MARSHMALLOW, OPENING AN UMBRELLA ON A WINDY DAY (this one is really hard to guess), and CLIMBING A WALL.

6. SPIN A STORY

Number of Players:	4–Unlimited
Age Range:	8–Adult
Preparation:	A bottle

The group sits on the floor in a circle. The leader sits in the center and explains that he is going to spin the bottle. When it stops, whoever it points to will begin telling a story.

To start with, the players are each asked to think of an exciting opening sentence, so that if they have to start, they will be prepared!

A typical story might start like this: "I was walking along the street, when I saw a small gold key under some leaves on the sidewalk. There was a note tied to the key, it said:" . . .

As soon as the first person starts to speak, the bottle spinner twists the bottle again. When it stops spinning, the next person starts to speak, continuing the story, which must make sense, each sentence following logically after the last one.

Storytellers should be prepared to stop in the middle of a sentence, and there should be only a minimal wait between speakers. If the next player pauses too long, he or she is out.

7. IN THE NEWS

Number of Players:	4–Unlimited
Age Range:	8–Adult
Preparation:	An assortment of printed words cut from magazines, comics, and newspapers

All the guests sit in a circle, and take turns coming up with a one-word headline, a word that will really attract attention, such as fire, storm, avalanche, holiday.

From the pile of cut-out words lying face down, each child takes four words. The child needs to create a headline from at least two of these words. If children agree, they may exchange words. For example, "I'll swap a DOG for a BEAR, or an OF for a NO." They get five minutes to prepare the headlines, and the completed ones, "MAN BITES DOG," or "BEAR HUNT OVER," should be read or called out as *dramatically* as possible.

8. PLAYFULLY

Number of Players:	4–30
Age Range:	8–Adult
Preparation:	Print a number of adverbs on slips of paper, three to a page:

ANGRILY	CHEERFULLY	TIREDLY
PLAYFULLY	MEANLY	HAPPILY
SOFTLY	LOVINGLY	PROUDLY

Divide the players into pairs or small groups, depending on the number of participants. Give each group a slip of paper on which three adverbs are printed. They are going to have to perform simple tasks in the style of the adverbs on the paper. They may do it as simply as walking "tiredly" across the room, or their performance may take the form of a more complex scene, such as showing a classroom in which everyone is tired. Talking is permitted, as long as the actual word is not given away. For example, if the adverb is tiredly, it would not be fair to say: "I feel so tired today!"

Give the groups a few minutes to discuss their words and then time them from the start of the first "scene," as the other groups watch. The other groups try to guess the adverb. As soon as the first word is guessed, the group proceeds to the next one. The first group to complete all the adverbs wins.

9. EXPERTS

Number of Players:	3–12
Age Range:	9–Adult
Preparation:	A chair or stool facing the group
	Funny, outrageous or unusual topics printed on cards
	Topics that have worked well with all kinds of age ranges include flea training, homework machine, baby talk, python power, "my new invention is."
	A small prize for the "most expert" expert

A volunteer chooses a topic from the pile of cards that is face down. Allow each player 15 seconds before starting for "thinking time." The volunteer must talk as long and as fluently as possible about the subject that is written on the card, without laughing or pausing. The speech must be audible, and may be

Ian, 7

followed by questions, which all should be answered. After everyone has a turn, the player cast their votes for the "best" expert and a prize is awarded.

A fun variation of this game is to have topics called out at random from the group; the same length of "thinking" time applies. In another variation, speeches could be timed, and a prize given for the longest one.

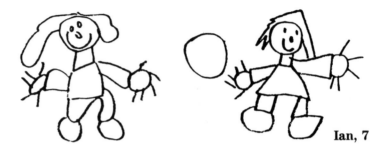

Ian, 7

10. MAKE A COMMERCIAL

Number of Players:	4–30
Age Range:	6–Adult
Preparation:	Some ordinary household objects in a bag or basket, hidden under a cloth: a bar of soap, a container of juice, a toothbrush, a pair of socks, a shoelace, a nail file, etc.
	Paper and pencils as needed
	Small prizes such as erasers, pencil sharpeners, keyrings

The guests decide whether they wish to work alone, in pairs, or in groups, on an original commercial. Then one person from each group takes an object from the hidden pile. The group has 10-15 minutes to prepare a commercial for the object. Contestants are encouraged to be as creative and unusual as possible. Extra points are awarded if the commercial is sung!

Prizes are awarded for the outstanding commercial, as decided by the audience.

11. HATS, PROPS, AND COSTUMES

Number of Players: 4–24

Age Range: 8–Adult

Preparation: A pile of clean newspapers—at least one complete paper per couple. (Brown wrapping paper is cleaner but more expensive.)

Scissors (one for every 4 people)

Masking or sticky tape

A wastebasket for scraps

Small prizes

This is a messy game! Children work in pairs or threes, and the object of the game is to make a costume out of newspaper and then to model it as in a fashion show in which one child models the costume and the other is the announcer ("Chef Philippe is wearing the latest in wraparound apron and chef's hat.") A prize is awarded for the most effective, or original costume.

In another version of the game, the leader asks participants to think of a famous couple or trio in the movies, cartoon, the news or literature—Prince Charles and Princess Di, for instance, or Little Red Riding Hood, the Wolf, and Grandma. Again, props and costume pieces are created to suggest the characters, but this time, the contestants make up a sentence, spoken in the style of the characters portrayed. In "Little Red Riding Hood," for example: "Oh, Grandma, what big teeth you have!" The rest of the guests must guess who they are. Again, prizes can be awarded for the best effort.

To Read Aloud:	*The Paper Bag Princess* by Robert Munsch *Anne of Green Gables* by Lucy M. Montgomery
Video:	*Big Red*—Walt Disney *Pete and the Dragon* (Musical)—Walt Disney
Snack Suggestions:	Decorate and bake prepared pizza slices. Have various toppings available, such as grilled sliced wieners, ham, cooked hamburger, onions, green pepper and sliced cheese. Fruit salad and cookies and ice cream. Have three or four sauces ready and top with whipped cream.
Invitations:	Cut out pictures of famous people and paste them on blank index cards. The invitations should specify that guests come dressed and made up as "Who you would like to be."

Halloween

Basic Motif: Ghosts, ghouls and witches
Where: Indoors

Andrew, 10

"Winnie the Pooh woke up suddenly in the middle of the night and listened. Then he got out of bed, and lit his candle ..."

A. A. Milne, *The World of Pooh*

1. MAKE A MASK

Number of Players:	1–25
Age Range:	6–Adult
Preparation:	Have one adult per 6 children, ready to give help with tricky bits, such as cutting eyeholes. Spread clean sheets of paper over a large flat surface, either a table or the floor. Allow one picnic paper plate per child, and a few to spare.
	Half squares of felt obtainable in any craft shop are also good for the basic mask. They have the added advantage of being soft to wear and are already in color.
	Pre-punch holes at the sides of the plate, and thread through string, wool or cord for fastening. This allows guests to concentrate on working on the fun part.
	Several pairs of scissors—one for four people
	Glue
	Pencils, chalk or crayons, and felt pens
	Basic materials to design the face: Wool, raffia, crepe hair, felt and fabric scraps, colored tissue paper, construction paper, pipe cleaners, buttons, beads and ribbon
	Have a trash bag or wastebasket close by.

When the guests arrive, lead them to the "design space" and encourage them to create their idea of a Halloween witch or wizard mask. The adult should be ready with a pencil or a piece of chalk to mark where the eyeholes come, and in general to assist younger children. When the mask is ready, fasten the strings securely.

Allow at least 20 minutes for this activity, in addition to clean-up and hand-washing time. When the masks are finished they can be worn for the next activity, which is a listening one, but should be removed for the active games (for safety reasons) and may be taken home.

Depending on the weather, a march around the yard wearing the completed disguise is a fun introduction to the theme of the party.

2. WELCOME

Number of Players:	2–Unlimited
Age Range:	6–12
Preparation:	A candle in a secure candle holder, lighter or matches
	A cassette tape recorder and appropriate tape, such as "The Sorcerer's Apprentice" by Dukas or "Danse Macabre" by Saint-Saens
	A book of scary poems or stories to read from
	A stool or chair for the reader

Wearing the masks they have just made, the children sit on the floor around the storyteller. The candle is lit, and mood music played softly in the background, while eerie stories or poems are read. With no light other than that of the candle, shadows are cast on the walls, and the masks and the words and music present a very ghostly atmosphere. It is not a good idea to allow this to go on too long, and the next game provides a lively contrast.

3. BOBBING FOR APPLES

Number of Players:	4–Unlimited
Age Range:	5–Adult
Preparation:	A plastic bowl, filled with water
	Paper towels
	One shiny red apple (preferably with stalk attached) for each contestant
	A card with a number printed on it for each participant, starting with #1
	A soft scarf

No Halloween party would be complete without this traditional winner.

Place the apples in the water-filled container. Each child chooses a card from the pile lying face down. The number on the card will determine the order in which the players will bob for apples.

Each contestant kneels down in front of the bowl, which stands on paper towels! Hands are loosely tied behind the players' back. Set a time limit of about 30 seconds to a minute, in which time the player tries to pick up the bobbing apple with his teeth, or mouth. Successful players keep the apple.

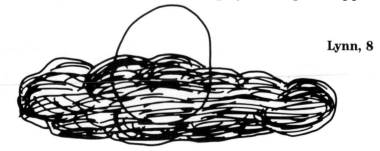

Lynn, 8

4. WITCH TAG

Number of Players:	4–25 (depending on the available space—outdoors is ideal)
Age Range:	6–Adult
Preparation:	Clear the space, or push back the furniture as much as possible. Children should remove their masks for safety.

One child is chosen as the Witch or Wizard, and becomes the tagger, who then decides and announces what kind of creature everyone is to become. For example: "You are all black cats," or spiders, goblins or night owls. After the game starts, when the tagger touches a player, that player must freeze instantly into the given shape, and must stay as that creature without moving until the end of the game. The last child caught becomes "IT." Three rounds are usually enough to wear out even the most energetic group!

5. BLOW OUT THE CANDLE

Number of Players:	3–15
Age Range:	6–Adult
Preparation:	An adult must be present beside the candle.
	A blindfold
	A small table
	A candle in a safe candle holder or stuck onto a saucer
	Matches or lighter

This game has been played throughout the centuries in many countries. The guests sit well out of the way, while they wait their turn. The candle is placed on the table and lit. Each contestant in turn is given a few moments to memorize the position of the candle. One child is then blindfolded and turned around a few times about two feet away from the candle. Her job is to find and blow out the candle—no hands allowed. Set a short time limit for this part (say 30 seconds). Once she locates the candle, she has three chances to blow out the flame. Adjust the position of the candle a little for each contestant, so as to provide a different challenge each time. Give everyone a turn.

6. DOUGHNUT GOBBLE

Number of Players:	2–Unlimited
Age Range:	5–Adult
Preparation:	One doughnut with a hole in the middle for every competitor
	A long piece of string
	Paper towels for each competitor
	A soft scarf for each competitor
	A small prize

Thread a piece of string through each doughnut, and suspend from a height, such as a staircase. Or, if you prefer, tie one long string through all the doughnuts and fasten each end to convenient hooks in the room. Place the paper towels beneath the doughnuts, in case they fall. Tie the competitors' hands behind them. On the word "Go" the players must try to eat the doughnuts as fast as possible. Doughnuts that fall on the napkins can be eaten, as long as hands are not used. The first player to finish eating the doughnut wins the prize.

7. GET YOUR APPLE

Number of Players:	4–25
Age Range:	6–Adult
Preparation:	A clean sheet, tablecloth or paper
	Shiny red apples—one per child
	Eerie or lively music (depending on the mood you want—Walt Disney's "The Haunted House" is a good choice)

A practice round is a good idea for this game. The apples, one *less* than there are players, are put on the cloth. When the music starts the children move around in time to the beat. The moment the music stops, everyone tries to grab an apple. As there are always fewer apples than children, one more player is eliminated each time. This continues until only one apple and two contestants remain. The last contestant who grabs the apple keeps it.

Anyone who takes an apple before the music stops is out. Children usually want to play this game several times.

8. FLASHLIGHT FACES

Number of Players:	6–Unlimited
Age Range:	6–Adult
Preparation:	Mood music, such as "A Saucer Full of Secrets," from "Ummagumma" by Pink Floyd
	A flashlight

The children sit in a circle, wearing their masks, if they wish. Lights are turned off, and music plays softly. A lighted flashlight is passed around, bulb up. When the music stops, who-ever is holding the flashlight—and whose face is therefore illuminated—is named by the circle and is out. The name can be the child's real name, or the one designated by the mask, "Dracula," for instance, or "Goblin."

Chris, 6

9. WAKE THE WITCH

Number of Players:	4–Unlimited
Age Range:	7–Adult
Preparation:	A shawl, a witch hat, or some costume piece that identifies the witch

This is an excellent outdoor game.

Teach the children the words of the following chant:

> A witch is sleeping
> Under the churchyard wall.
> Be careful when you see her
> And run when you hear her call.

One child becomes the "Witch," who sits leaning against a wall, with eyes closed. As wide a space as possible separates the Witch from the safe area or "Home" where the players wait. The game begins with the chanting children going as close to the Witch as they dare. The Witch is allowed to open her eyes on the word "careful." On the last line of the song, she may get up, and as soon as the word "call" is spoken, she runs after the chanters and tries to catch as many as possible before they get "Home" and to safety. She calls, "Come here, come here," as she chases them. Any child touched is out, and the last one caught is the new Witch.

Ian, 7

10. LET ME OUT

Number of Players:	6–Unlimited
Age Range:	7–Adult
Preparation:	A small sheet of white tablecloth

A standing circle is formed around the "Ghost." The children hold hands tightly. The circle symbolizes the walls of the haunted house. (Walls may creak and groan, but they don't giggle.) The object of the game is to stop the Ghost from getting out, and the game is most effective when the circle is silent. The child who is chosen to be the Ghost crouches in the center of the circle, covered with the sheet. Ghosts should be told they can take off the sheet if they feel uncomfortable in any way. When the leader signals that the circle is ready, the Ghost stands up, and says "Let me out," and then attempts to break out of the circle. There should be no response to the ghost, who is allowed to make spooky sounds and noises. Set a time limit of 25–30 seconds for the ghost. Everyone who wants to be the Ghost gets a turn.

11. GHOST STORY

Number of Players:	4–Unlimited
Age Range:	7–Adult
Preparation:	A flashlight
	The "Ghost Sheet," a small white sheet, shawl, or cloth

This game makes a wonderful campfire activity.

The children form a circle, including the leader, who holds the flashlight. The Ghost Sheet is draped around the leader like a shawl. Lights are switched off so that the only light is that of the fire and flashlight, which shines up on the leader's face. The leader begins a ghost story, with a sentence to spark the imagination, for example: "In the graveyard the bones pushed their way out of the earth, suddenly . . ." or "I was alone in the room, when, suddenly, the skeleton in the corner started to sing and sway . . ."

The leader should choose an opening sentence that is appropriate for the age and interests of the guests. A little bit of being scared, even in safe surroundings, goes a long way!

At the point in the sentence or story when it is most interesting, the Ghost Sheet is handed on, and the next person continues with the story. The leader beams the flashlight onto this child, who adds a word, a sound, or some sentences to the story. Children may contribute as little or as much as they wish. The Ghost Sheet is handed on again as soon as the storyteller of the moment finishes his contribution.

After everyone has had a turn, anyone may volunteer to start the story and beam the flashlight.

For a variation, the leader sits in the center, and after the opening sentence, beams the flashlight at *random*. Whoever is "in the light" carries the story forward. The flashlight must move rapidly.

12. RHYMING SPELLS

Number of Players:	6–Unlimited
Age Range:	8–Adult
Preparation:	Pencil and paper and small prizes

Divide the guests into groups of three, four or five. Give them 10–15 minutes to decide on a spell. Any kind of spell is fine—to make yourself invisible, for instance, to turn an enemy into a frog, or to turn sand into gold. That part is easy, and the groups will have lots of ideas, but the spell has to *rhyme*. After the group has made up the spell, the children need to decide on the most effective way to present it. They may choose to chant, sing, divide up the lines, and even add actions. Winners are decided by democratic vote. A small prize is awarded to each member of the winning group.

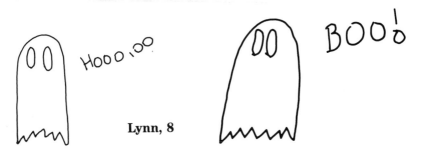

Lynn, 8

To Read Aloud:	*The Sorcerer's Apprentice* by Robin Muller *Who's Afraid? and Other Strange Stories* by Philippa Pearce
Video:	*Disney Halloween Treat* (classic scenes from Disney)
Snack Suggestions:	Barbecued chicken wings or mini-wieners in puff pastry. Baked potatoes with a choice of toppings, such as chili or cheese. Coleslaw, miniature wiener rolls, apple crumb cake or pumpkin pie and ice cream. Chocolate chip cookies.
Invitations:	A cut-out white paper ghost pasted on colored cardboard.

Winter

Ian, 6

SMALL BOY: *When you were a boy what was*
    Christmas like?
SELF: *It snowed.*
SMALL BOY: *It snowed last year, too. I made a snow-*
    man and my brother knocked it down, and I
    knocked my brother down, and then we had tea.

Dylan Thomas, *Conversations About Christmas*

1. WINTER BIRDS

Number of Players:	4–Unlimited
Age Range:	5–Adult
Preparation:	Cut out shapes of birds from red and green cardboard or construction paper. Hide the shapes well around the party area.

As the children arrive, tell them that cut-out birds are hidden in the party area. They are to find just one and keep it. Its color will determine whether they will be on the "red" or the "green" team. It's fun to watch each new arrival and wait to see whose team they'll be on.

Angel, 8

2. WHAT DOES THE SNOWMAN SAY? NOTHING!

Number of Players:	5–Unlimited
Age Range:	5–Adult
Preparation:	A hat, preferably a bowler hat
	A muffler

One child, the Snowman, dressed up in the hat and muffler, stands stiffly facing the group. He must not respond in any way—by giggling, moving or speaking. The object of the game is for the children to get a reply to their questions, such as "What's your middle name?" "Who's your best friend?" "Do you like ice cream?", or to make the Snowman laugh by making faces. No touching is allowed. Establish a short time limit, and play several times. Any child who gets a response from the Snowman, becomes the next one. Finish up with a *SNOW-MELT*: Everyone turns into a Snowman and at a signal "the sun comes out," and the Snowmen begin to "melt down" to the floor—the *last* one to melt completely (stretch out on the floor) is the winner. *Rule:* Keep moving all the time.

3. DUCKS AND PTARMIGANS

Number of Players:	4–Unlimited (depending on space)
Age Range:	6–Adult
Preparation:	A large space, ideally played outside

This is a favorite game of the Inuits, Eskimo people who live in northern Canada. It is still played in the Winter Games, in Inuvik, Northwest Territories in Canada.

Children line up in two teams (eight to ten per side is a good size. If you have a larger group, you can play the game in shifts, or more than two teams can play simultaneously).

One team, the red birds, which are the Ptarmigans—represent winter and the setting sun. The green birds—the Ducks—represent the coming of spring.

The team leaders face each other across a designated line, their teams lined up behind them. The team leaders grasp each others hands, and each team member holds onto the person in front (arms around waists) tightly. On a given signal the tug of war begins. There is a strict time limit of not more than 30 seconds. The "season" that pulls the other side across the line wins.

If the teams are very unequal in size, the leader can call "SCRAMBLE," and the teams rearrange themselves.

4. THE TOY SHOP

Number of Players:	2–Unlimited
Age Range:	5–Adult
Preparation:	Place 12–15 small toys on a table or floor.
	Small cars, dolls, playing cards, jacks, marbles, crayons, paints, plasticine, puzzles, comics, etc. Several toys of the same type make the game more difficult.

A volunteer goes out, or faces a wall while the toys are re-arranged, and one item is removed. The volunteer must guess correctly which toy is gone. Only one guess is allowed. Repeat this several times, so that several children get a turn. Everyone wants to try it, so play as many times as possible without getting bogged down.

For a really sharp group, try a more difficult version of the game. Rearrange two of the toys. The volunteer must not only guess which ones were moved but also has to put them back in their original position.

5. MUSICAL CANDY

Number of Players:	6–Unlimited
Age Range:	5–Adult
Preparation:	Small paper plates
	Wrapped candies, one for each player
	Live or taped music

Place the paper plates at intervals around the room, with lots of space between each one. There is one less plate than there are competitors. Each child is given a wrapped candy. As the music plays, the children move around the room. When it stops, each child attempts to place a candy (one to a plate only) on a plate. Since there are fewer plates than candies, one child and one candy are out. After each round one more plate is taken away until only one plate and two contestants remain. The winner is allowed to eat the piece of candy. This game needs to be played several times. Music should be played in short bursts. *Rule:* No pushing.

6. FILL THE STOCKINGS

Number of Players:	4–16
Age Range:	6–Adult
Preparation:	Four large stockings or small paper bag or loot bags.
	An assortment of small objects (preferably each team gets the same *size*, as well as number of objects—4 hats, 4 balls, 4 flashlights, 4 umbrellas, etc.)

The guests assemble into four teams. Each team is given the

same number of objects to fit into a sock or bag. It should not be too easy to fit the things into the container. On the word GO, each team starts to pack up the objects as securely as possible. Then one member of each team must carry the full bag to a designated place in the room, without spilling or dropping the contents. Whichever team does it first is the winner. Of course, if the bag breaks, or drops, the team must start all over again. This really tests its skill and speed.

7. WHAT'S IN THE PARCEL?

Number of Players:	6–Unlimited
Age Range:	5–Adult
Preparation:	An object of unusual shape—a shoe horn, for instance, or a trumpet, a candlestick, a pie dish, a fat cushion
	Wrapping paper or cloth
	String or ribbon
	Taped or live music
	A small prize

Children sit in a circle on the floor or on chairs. The oddly shaped object, securely wrapped in paper or cloth, is passed around. There is a time limit for each child to feel the parcel— a slow count of five by those watching: "1000, 2000, 3000, 4000, 5000" and so on—and pass the parcel. When everyone has had a turn to feel the parcel the guessing starts. This continues until someone guesses correctly. *Then* the parcel is passed around once more, this time to music. When the music stops (very short turns are the most fun), the child holding the parcel starts the unwrapping process. This continues around the circle until the object appears. Only then is the prize awarded to the child who originally guessed the object. In case of a tie, more than one prize is awarded.

8. WRAP THE GIFTS

Number of Players:	6–16
Age Range:	6–Adult
Preparation:	This is an excellent way to use up all those odd bits of gift wrap.

Sticky tape

Scissors

Newspaper

String or ribbon

Boxes and containers of all shapes and sizes, one per guest

Felt pens

Taped or live music

If the party is mixed in age, make up teams that are balanced in age range. Give one box or container to each team member to gift wrap. At a signal, all start to wrap, and the first team to finish neatly wrapping all the "gifts" and label each package "to _____" wins. It really helps the energy if Christmas music is played.

Andrea, 9

9. CAROLLING

Number of Players:	4–Unlimited
Age Range:	6–Adult
Preparation:	Song sheets with at least six popular carols or seasonal songs on them—for instance, "Rudolf the Red-Nosed Reindeer," "I'm Dreaming of a White Christmas," "Silent Night," "Jingle Bells"

Each team is given one sheet for every two or three children. The print should be easy to read. The teams are given a few minutes to decide which song they would like to sing, and they are given a little time to practise, preferably not all in the same room. It doesn't matter at all, if more than one team chooses the same song! All the teams entertain each other, and there is lots of applause, and perhaps encores.

10. WINTER SCENES

Number of Players:	4–Unlimited
Age Range:	6–Adult
Preparation:	In a shoe box arrange four or five objects—all related, except one. For example, on white tissue paper or cotton, arrange a tiny mirror (representing a pond), a small tree or piece of driftwood, a tiny bird, a doll or animal, and a toy helicopter, engine, or car.

Group the children into twos or threes. Each group is given a few minutes to look at the contents of the "Winter Scene."

Then five minutes or a little longer is allowed for the groups to invent a story about the objects. The only rule is that each object must be logically accounted for. Children hold the box as they tell their stories.

In an interesting variation each team gets a shoe box, many kinds of crafts materials, and an assortment of tiny objects such as shells, animals, flowers, figures, and miniature toys. They are given a time limit to create their own winter wonderland. The most original scene gets a team prize.

Andrew, 10

11. THE FORGOTTEN CARD

Number of Players: 2–Unlimited

Age Range: 5–Adult

Preparation: Construction paper cut into different shapes

Prepasted paper such as ORIGAMI

Tissue paper

Glitter

Sequins

Scraps of silk, satin or cotton fabric

Cotton

Ribbon

Crayons

Felt markers

Pencils

Glue and sticky tape

Scissors

Newspaper

Put down newspaper on the floor and sort all the craft materials into piles on a table, so that they are easily accessible. Children are asked to think about someone who may not get many cards, such as a lonely senior citizen who may not have grandchildren. Each child creates a card, which may be taken home.

The children may decide—it would be a kind thought—to mail the cards to a local hospital or home, or the leader can arrange for the children to distribute them personally.

12. LUCKY DIP

Number of Players:	2–Unlimited
Age Range:	4–Adult
Preparation:	Tree decorations, wrapped in foil, colored tissue or holiday gift wrap
	A small tree or large branch
	A wicker basket or container
	Numbers from 1–20 (or whatever size of group is playing)

The wrapped-up tree decorations are put into a basket. Guests draw a number and then proceed, in numerical order to pick a package, which they unwrap right away. The tree decorations may be taken home by each child, or the guests may help to decorate a small tree or branch that can be used in school, or given to the local hospital children's ward. *Rule:* Everyone waits for each gift to be unwrapped before the next one is picked.

Ian, 7

To Read Aloud:	"A Chanukah Eve in Warsaw" from *Naftali: the Storyteller and His Horse, Sus* by Isaac Bashevis Singer *The Snowman* by Raymond Briggs
Video:	*A Christmas Carol* or *A Christmas Story*—Walt Disney
Snack Suggestions:	Small sandwiches filled with cheese spread, salami, egg salad, tuna salad Gingerbread cookie men cut in the shapes of trees, stars, birds Fruit jello and ice cream A cake cut in the shape of a Christmas tree and decorated with white frosting "snow."
Invitations:	A card in the shape of a snowman with a bowler hat on his head and a carrot nose.

Animals

Basic Motif: Pets and other creatures
Where: Indoor/Outdoor

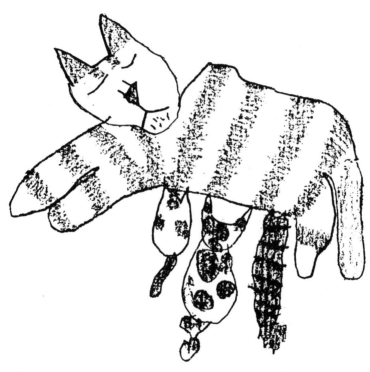

Ian, 7

"When I grow up I'm going to have 16 cats and 1 dog."

Mandy, 10

1. FIND THE ANIMAL

Number of Players:	2–Unlimited
Age Range:	4–Adult
Preparation:	Cut pictures of animals from newspapers and magazines, and glue them to index cards to prevent their curling up at the edges.
	Print the names of the animals on separate strips of paper or cards.

Hide the pictures and the names of the animals separately, in a clearly defined area. For under-7s hide only the pictures. On arrival each child is told which animal to find. Jane, for instance, is told a rabbit. She may see several other pictures before she finds her rabbit, but she must not tell anyone where they are or even which animal she is looking for. Younger children love the idea of secrets, and it's fun to watch the new arrivals looking for their animal pictures; it helps to fill the time until everyone has arrived. Very young children accompanied by an adult may certainly work with Mother or Father as a partner.

2. WHO AM I?

Number of Players:	5–25
Age Range:	5–Adult
Preparation:	None

The children sit on the floor in a circle, close their eyes and think of an animal (Suggest the one on their picture, if they can't think of one immediately.). Then they open their eyes, and each child in turn, makes the sound of the chosen animal. The circle guesses what animal it is. If the first guess is not correct, another clue is added with gesture and movement, to make the animal clearer. A cat, for instance, could purr, arch its back, and show its claws.

3. SNAKE IN THE GRASS

Number of Players:	4–Unlimited
Age Range:	4–10
Preparation:	One long glove or mitten. Buttons for eyes (optional)

One child volunteers to be a snake, puts on a long glove and lies face down on the floor. The other children approach the snake, and, to see whether it's asleep, gently prod it with one finger only. When the leader calls "Snake in the grass," the snake, without getting to its feet, must tag as many children as possible. The last child to be tagged becomes the new snake.

Rules: Establish a very clearly marked boundary beyond which no one is allowed to run. Each snake has a time limit of one minute.

Jay, 8

4. HUNT THE DEER

Number of Players:	6–25
Age Range:	6–Adult
Preparation:	A blindfold

All the children stand in a circle, and become Trees. When the game starts, the Trees may make very soft sounds like wind rustling though leaves, but they may not talk or giggle, which would make it too hard for the hunter to hear.

Andrew, 10

One child, the Hunter, is blindfolded. A second child, the Deer, joins the Hunter in the middle of the circle and tries to keep from being caught by the Hunter. The Deer may play tricks by making a sound with voice or feet, and then moving quickly to another spot in the circle. The trees gently guide the Hunter back if he gets out of the circle by mistake. There is a 30-second time limit for the game. One touch means the deer is caught. Play the game enough times so that everyone who wants to gets a chance to be either Hunter or Deer. The children may change the name of the animal each time: The Deer could be a lion, a shark, or even a frog!

In a variation on the game the leader gives the "animal" a small bell or noisemaker to hold, which the Hunter follows.

5. KANGAROOS FLY

Number of Players:	4–Unlimited
Age Range:	4–8
Preparation:	None

The game begins by the leader asking the group "What kind of things fly?" The children will probably answer "Birds," or helicopters or butterflies. The next question might be: "Do snakes fly? Bats? Elephants? Ants?"

Then the leader explains the object of the game. Standing in front of the group, the leader waves his arms while making a statement such as, "All sparrows fly." Everyone copies the action. The aim of the game, is to trick the players into waving their arms even when the statement is untrue. "All kangaroos fly." (Untrue). "All ducks fly." (True). The leader may name any animal, object or word. Players who raise their arms by mistake are out. The leader who manages to get most people out in a round is the winner.

Practice rounds are a good idea with this age group.

6. NURSERY RHYMES

Number of Players:	6–Unlimited
Age Range:	5–Adult
Preparation:	Nursery rhymes with animals in them printed on special sheets—one per group
	For instance: "Baa baa, black sheep," "Little boy blue," "Three blind mice," "Hey, diddle diddle, the cat and the fiddle," "Little Miss Muffet" (optional)

Divide the children into small groups of 3–6 players. Ask each team to think of a nursery rhyme with an animal in it, or let them choose one from the sheet of rhymes. Give the groups a

Jaclyn, 8

62

few minutes to agree on a rhyme, and make a plan for acting out the poem without any words being spoken. Only action is allowed. The other groups must guess which animal, or animals they are pantomiming, and the name of the nursery rhyme.

7. ANIMAL MASKS

Number of Players:	2–25 (Remember to allow one helper for every six children.)
Age Range:	5–Adult
Preparation:	One plain colored picnic plate per child (and a few extras, in case of accidents). Eyeholes may be precut and holes punched in the side with string or twine knotted through for fastening. Each plate has *one* feature already added, such as felt ears, wool whiskers, a red nose.
	Fun craft materials: Corks, buttons, sequins, glitter, wool, pipe cleaners, scraps of cotton, silk or velvet
	Masking tape and paper glue
	Scissors (one for every two children)
	Staplers
	Felt pens, crayons
	Newspaper
	A trash bag or wastebasket

Spread newspaper on the floor or table. Distribute the craft materials neatly, so that the children don't need to fight over them. Everyone chooses a plate, which already has some "character" added to it, and then decorates the mask fully. The guests may take the masks home.

8. MEOW, KITTY, MEOW

Number of Players: 4–25

Age Range: 5–Adult

Preparation: A blindfold

Everyone sits in a circle. One child stands in the middle, blind-folded. The leader turns him around two or three times. He points to anyone in the circle, who then replies "Meow, kitty, meow." The child who is blindfolded must guess who the voice belongs to. If he is correct, they trade places. No one is blindfolded for more than three turns. If the group is quite large, and some children don't know each other very well, take time before the game starts, for everyone to listen to each child speak their real name and say a few words—"I'm Tiffany, I like cats," for example. This will make the game a little easier.

9. WHERE'S MY TAIL?

Number of Players: 2–Unlimited

Age Range: 5–Adult

Preparation: A blindfold

A large drawing or picture of a cat or a rabbit, minus a tail, mounted on a thick piece of cardboard or corkboard

A piece of wool, string, or ribbon attached to a tack, one for each guest. For a rabbit picture, use a piece of · white felt for the tail.

A small prize

The animal picture minus a tail is mounted on corkboard, and put on the wall at child height. Each child takes turns being blindfolded and then tacking the "tail" on the animal. The players are given 30 seconds to look at the picture before being blindfolded. Children should be placed quite close to the corkboard to have their turn, and it helps if the leader initials each attempt (to prevent arguments). There is a prize for the closest placing of the tail.

10. PRICKLY PORCUPINE

Number of Players:	6–Unlimited
Age Range:	6–Adult
Preparation:	A large outline of a porcupine *without prickles*, one per group
	One picture of porcupine *with prickles*
	Crayons or felt pens
	A prize for each team member

Show the children the picture of the porcupine. Then divide them into small groups of 3–5. Give each team member a crayon or felt pen and one animal outline. The object of the game is to fill in the porcupine's prickles, without leaving space between. The prickles *must* be drawn vertically: |||||(((|||/ . The first team to completely fill in the outline with prickles wins the contest, and is awarded a prize.

This game can also be played very successfully individually. Just give each child an outline drawing and crayons or a pen and play in the same way.

Treena, 9

11. PUPPET STORY

Number of Players: 4–30

Age Range: 4–10

Preparation: An animal hand or finger puppet, which may range from a mouse to a lion

Children sit in a circle. The leader sits in the circle with them and puts on the puppet. Before the story begins, the leader asks some questions: "Who is this character?" "Where does he live?" "What does he like to eat?" "Does he have a friend?" "Is he going to have an adventure?"

The replies will not only help start the story, but will give the players ideas, for when their turn comes around.

The leader's opening sentence could go like this: "One day a rabbit was sneaking down a path, looking for a friend to play with, when suddenly he saw an enormous ..." At this exciting moment, the leader hands the puppet to the next child in the circle, who may add as much to the story as she wants. One word is just as acceptable as one sentence. The leader should be prepared with more questions, or ready to link words to help move the story along. Everyone enjoys having an opportunity to wear the puppet and be part of the story. This is a quiet and comfortable conclusion to a high energy party, before snacks or going home. It could work well for younger children, as an alternative to reading a story or watching a video.

Catherine

To Read Aloud:	*Can You Catch Josephine?* by Stephane Poulin *A Bear Called Paddington* by Michael Bond
Video:	*Bambi* or *101 Dalmatians* or *Benjy*—Walt Disney
Snack Suggestions:	Bacon, lettuce and tomato sandwiches or bacon, pineapple and cheese toasted sandwiches, either kind cut in "fingers." Cream cheese and celery sticks. Chocolate cupcakes with animal designs in frosting. Fresh fruit salad and frozen yogurt or ice cream.
Invitations:	A cut-out felt silhouette of an animal glued on an index card.

Valentine

Basic Motif: Friendship   **Where:** Indoors

Amy, 10

"I'll give my love an apple without a core
I'll give my love a house without a door
I'll give my love a palace where she may be
And she may unlock it without a key."

Anon

1. VALENTINE COUNTDOWN

Number of Players:	2–Unlimited
Age Range:	4–Adult
Preparation:	Jelly beans and candies—generous quantities
	Decorated paper cups, cones, or miniature valentine baskets

On arrival, each guest is handed a cup, cone or container, and told to find the special candies that are hidden around the party space. The children are each allowed 25 seconds to find as many candies as possible. Everyone watches the search, counting aloud. Children who prefer may trade their candies in for nickels and dimes.

2. STEP ON MY HEART

Number of Players:	6–Unlimited
Age Range:	5–Adult
Preparation:	Large cut-out paper hearts; newsprint painted red is ideal. The hearts should be big enough to hold several people standing. Have six hearts minimum for 12 guests.
	Taped music with an appropriate theme such as "My Funny Valentine"
	Stickers for prizes

Place the paper hearts on the floor, leaving sufficient floor space around them for guests to walk. Partners are decided at random before the game by just counting off from 1–12, and asking the children to find an odd or even number for a partner.

When the music starts, partners, who must hold hands, start walking around the floor space. When the music stops, everyone tries to stand on a heart. Partners may not be separated, and if even a small part of one partner's foot is not on the heart, the couple is out. As players are eliminated, remove hearts until only one remains. A trial round is strongly recommended. Winners are presented with a sticker in the shape of a heart.

3. SIT ON MY KNEE

Number of Players:	6–Unlimited
Age Range:	5–Adult
Preparation:	Cushions of different sizes, large enough to sit on. Place them around the room, one cushion for each pair of contestants, but one *less* than needed.
	Taped or live music

Guests choose a partner, but if this game is played immediately after the preceding one, make sure everyone changes partners so that all the guests get the opportunity to mix. The object of the game is to have fun and get everyone relaxed.

When the music starts, guests dance with each other. When it stops, the couples have only five seconds to find a cushion and sit down, one on the other's knee. Only one hand or foot is allowed to touch the floor. Anyone without a cushion or touching the floor in any way other than according to the rules, is out. One cushion is removed for each disqualified couple after each round. Depending on the size of cushions, competitors have been known to cram several bodies on to one cushion!

To make the game more fun, when the leader calls out "Change," everyone has five seconds to find a new partner and continue dancing until the music stops.

4. I SENT MY LOVE A VALENTINE

Number of Players: 6–Unlimited

Age Range: 6–Adult

Preparation: An envelope addressed TO MY VALENTINE

The children sit or stand in a circle facing inward for this traditional favorite. The "Singer" is given the envelope, walks around the *outside* of the circle, chanting:

> "I sent a letter to my love,
> On the way I dropped it.
> One of you has picked it up
> And put it in your pocket.
> It wasn't you, it wasn't you. ... etc.,
> It was you!"

The Singer drops the envelope behind the "chosen one" on the last "*you*" of the refrain. That person picks up the envelope and tries to catch the Singer before he can manage to steal her place in the circle. To make the contest a little more even, the Singer has to run around the circle one more time (counterclockwise); he cannot just sit down. If the Singer is tagged, he has to go on trying to get rid of the valentine, but if he reaches the vacated place safely, the new person takes over.

5. ONE WORD VALENTINE

Number of Players: 6–Unlimited

Age Range: 6–Adult

Preparation: Pencil and paper

To start the game off, everyone sits in a big circle. One person is chosen to begin the valentine by saying just one word,

"DEAR," for example. The next person in the circle adds, "MOTHER." The next says, "THANKS," and so on: 4. "FOR" 5. "HELPING" 6. "ME" 7. "OUT" 8. "WITH" 9. "MY" 10. "PAPER" 11. "ROUTE," etc.—until the valentine is completed. Anyone who hesitates, repeats a word, or uses more than one word is out.

Next, the children choose groups of five or six, and one person on each team is selected to write the message down. Each group makes up a valentine in exactly the same way as they did it in the circle. This time, though, the completed valentines are read aloud to other groups. There are usually some very funny results.

6. PICTURE VALENTINE

Number of Players:	4–Unlimited
Age Range:	6–Adult
Preparation:	Slip of paper with name of person at party or in community
	Blank index cards, one for each player
	Cut-out colored pictures of animals, flowers, scenes, children and delicious foods
	Print adjectives on index cards or paper, such as HAPPY, PRETTY, GENEROUS, LOVELY, KIND, NICE, etc.

Everyone receives a blank index card with a slip of paper stating who it is for. It will probably be for someone in the group, but it could be for someone else in the school or community. Allow as much time as you like for the children to select a picture and a suitable adjective or two from the previously prepared pile of cut-out pictures and words to paste on the card. As all these are complimentary, this should be fun and a happy experience. The leader may show the completed valentines and read them out (Of course, writers will remain anonymous!) or the guests might enjoy showing off the cards they received, and reading them out. It's a wonderful "lift" for the child who might not otherwise get a special card.

7. SO MANY WORDS

Number of Players:	2–Unlimited
Age Range:	8–Adult
Preparation:	Pencil and paper for each couple Written on the paper is: SWEETHEART and VALENTINE'S DAY

Children pair up with the partner of their choice. Each couple is given a piece of paper with two words written at the head of a column: SWEETHEART, VALENTINE'S DAY.

The first pair to write twelve words, made from the word SWEETHEART wins.

For example:

TREE	SEAT	WAS	SWEET
WEST	HATE	RAT	HEART
EAT	REST	HE	THEATRE
TRASH	WASH	THREE	

This may be repeated with the same partner for VALENTINE'S DAY. The winner is the couple who can make the greatest number of new words in a time limit of three minutes.

Ian, 7

8. MARRIAGE PROPOSAL

Number of Players:	4–Unlimited
Age Range:	7–Adult
Preparation:	Small prizes for the winners (two or three)

This game is played in partners. If numbers are unequal, it can make the situation even funnier. Partners are given ten minutes to prepare a marriage proposal for part of an imaginary television program: a foreign station mini-series, an historical romance; an old-fashioned movie with subtitles, or a soap opera. Then they get to act it out. Any style, language or format is okay. They can even sing it in operatic style. The more outrageous and funny, the better the chance of winning! The only rule is that the actors must not laugh; they must be serious or they are disqualified. The winners are chosen by a show of hands, and prizes are awarded.

Janine, 8

9. VALENTINE MIME RELAY

Number of Players: 6–30

Age Range: 6–Adult

Preparation: Mime activities printed on separate slips of paper, in keeping with the theme of the party. (See below.) One title for each team member.

This game is a popular one adapted from the mimes in "I Want To Be." Have the guests form teams of 10 or less, and give each player a number. You can have three or more teams. Then #One from each team goes up to the leader and is shown the piece of paper with the first mime on it. Instructions can also be whispered if there is a problem with reading. Then the #Ones return to their teams, and mime the activity. Warn everyone not to shout out the answer in their excitement, because that would give the answer away to the other teams. The child who is miming the word is not allowed to speak in answers to questions. All answers must be non-verbal! Contestants continue acting the word, adding clues until someone guesses correctly. Then #Two goes up to the leader, whispers the answer and is shown the next task.

The first team to complete all the mimes, and sit down in the original numerical order wins.

Some mimes that fit in with the Valentine theme are: Writing a letter; baking a cake; decorating a cake; picking a bouquet of flowers; receiving a big box of candy; dressing up in a party outfit; serenading a loved one under a window; refusing a proposal of marriage.

Ian, 7

10. IMPOSSIBLE HEARTS

Number of Players:	2–Unlimited
Age Range:	5–Adult
Preparation:	Paper and red crayons or felt markers
	Blindfolds as necessary

Each child is given a piece of paper and a red crayon or felt marker. Eyes are kept tightly closed for this game, which is quite difficult to do. On the word "GO", all the competitors must try to draw an outline of a heart, and color it in. There is a small prize for the most recognizable effort.

If the numbers are quite small—say, a group of six—it's fun to do the drawings one at a time, so that the others can watch. They may or may not make comments, such as "You've nearly finished," or "You're going too close to the edge of the paper."

11. HEART MOSAIC

Number of Players:	4–Unlimited
Age Range:	5–Adult
Preparation:	Outline drawings of a heart—one between two people
	Origami paper, pre-pasted, cut up in small uneven pieces, in containers, such as empty yogurt containers

Children choose partners and are given an outline of a heart, along with a container of small scraps of gummed red paper. At a signal to start, each team starts filling in the heart outline with the paper scraps. The first couple to totally cover the heart outline, *without going over the edge* and with no white paper showing, wins.

To Read Aloud:	*The Steadfast Tin Soldier* by Hans Christian Andersen *Sarah, Plain and Tall* by Patricia MacLachlan
Video:	*The Lady and the Tramp*— Walt Disney *Cinderella*—Walt Disney
Snack Suggestions:	Roast beef sandwiches, bologna sandwiches and potato salad. Tomato and cucumber salad. Mexican wedding cookies (the recipe is below) or heart-shaped cookies. Strawberry shortcake with whipped cream or vanilla ice cream and raspberry sauce. Pink lemonade.

MEXICAN WEDDING COOKIES:

¼ cup butter
¼ cup shortening
1 T sugar
½ t vanilla
1 cup flour
½ cup chopped walnuts
3 T confectioner's sugar

Cream butter, shortening and sugar. Add vanilla, flour and nuts. Mix well. Roll into small balls. Cook on ungreased cookie sheet for 15 minutes in 400° oven. Roll in confectioner's sugar while warm. Makes 15–18 cookies.

Invitations:	In the shape of a bookmark, with a small heart on the top, and details of the party theme underneath.

Balloons

Basic Motif: A simple object and lots of imagination
Where: Indoor/Outdoor

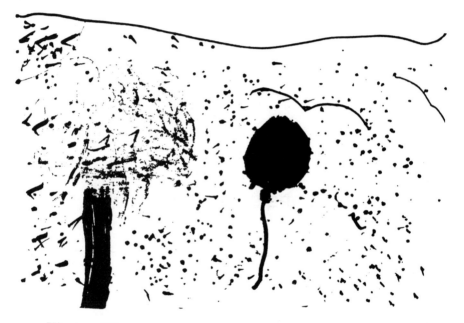

Kirsten, 6½

PAISLEY: *I like striped balloons with long bumpy shapes.*

JOHN: *It can pop, and you can kick it and play with it outside.*

PAISLEY: *And it's soft and if it hits somebody it doesn't hurt.*

SHELAGH: *I LIKE the balloons that are in the sky.*

Paisley, 8; John, 5; Shelagh, 3

1. FIND THE BALLOON

Number of Players:	2–Unlimited
Age Range:	4–Adult
Preparation:	One balloon per child (and a couple to spare, in case of accidents)
	Balloons may be of any color, shape or size
	A balloon pump (optional)

Uninflated balloons are hidden well in the party area. When the children arrive, they are asked to find one balloon of a particular color or shape. The leader could say, for example, "Your special balloon is green and it is long and thin." Other balloons should be left in their hiding places. As soon as each guest has found the correct balloon, an adult should be available if necessary, depending on the age of the child, to help blow up the balloon and tie it securely. Balloon pumps are invaluable, if the group is very large.

2. FLOATING BALLOONS

Number of Players:	2–Unlimited (depending on space)
Age Range:	4–Adult
Preparation:	One blown-up balloon for each player

The object of the game is to keep balloons up in the air, without letting them touch the floor. Start off by allowing the competitors to practise for a few minutes, and then give the signal for all the contestants to throw their balloons up in the air, and keep them floating, by whatever means. Any part of the body may be used, but no one is allowed to push anyone else, or touch another balloon. Once a balloon hits the ground, that player is eliminated. The last player left is the winner. Play several times.

3. BALLOON RACE

Number of Players:	2–Unlimited
Age Range:	5–Adult
Preparation:	A blown-up balloon for each player

Players decide on a starting line and a finishing line. Then they all stand behind the starting line. The object of the game is to get your balloon over the finish line first, but you have to get it there without using your hands to help it along. You may nudge it with your head or elbows, blow on it gently, push it with your feet—anything is permitted *except* hands. Naturally, if a balloon is touched, even by accident, the owner is eliminated.

This game needs a lot of energy, contortion and ingenuity!

4. CIRCUS SEALS

Number of Players:	6–Unlimited
Age Range:	5–Adult
Preparation:	One balloon for each team

The children are divided into teams of between two and six members. Each group is given one balloon. The object of the game is for the groups to keep the balloon in the air—it must not touch the floor. However, the decision as to *how* this is to be done is made by a Caller. Once each team has thrown its balloon in the air, the Caller treats the competitors rather like circus seals, and he chooses different parts of the body to call out—"Noses" or "Elbows," "Hips," or "Foreheads." The teams must obey and for as long as that particular body part has been called, nothing else may be used to keep the balloon in the air. It's a good idea for the Caller to change the part frequently. When the Caller shouts "Flippers," that is the *only* time when hands are allowed, and groups should make the most of it! If a balloon touches the floor, the whole group is out. A couple of practice rounds may be necessary, and the Caller can be changed often.

5. BALLOON FACE

Number of Players:	2–Unlimited
Age Range:	5–12
Preparation:	A balloon and a felt marker for each guest
	Balloons must be inflated

Every child is handed a balloon and a felt marker, and asked to draw a picture of an animal, a fictional character, a monster or

outer space creature—even a worm—anything they like. Be sure to remind them that balloons burst easily, so they should press very gently. Have replacement balloons ready just in case. Then the leader pairs up the balloons along with their creators (or groups them in threes), and the children create skits about what might happen if their characters met. A mouse, for example, might encounter a caterpillar and a dinosaur. Children will need about ten minutes to prepare their dialogue.

A table (on its side) or a chalkboard makes a perfectly acceptable puppet stage.

6. BALLOON STORY

Number of Players:	4–30
Age Range:	5–12
Preparation:	One inflated balloon (and one to spare) in any color or shape
	a felt marker with a broad tip

This is the game referred to in "Before You Begin," which, because of the "wait" for turns, and the suspense of "will we get around the circle without bursting the balloon?" is always a huge success.

Children sit in a circle. The balloon and marker are passed around the circle and each child can make any kind of mark or design. Remind them again that if they press too hard with the felt marker the balloon will burst. When the tip of the felt pen leaves the surface of the balloon, the turn is over. Everyone always watches very carefully for this!

When the balloon has been passed around the whole circle, the leader holds up the finished balloon and asks questions: "Who is it?" or "What does it remind you of?" Answers have ranged from "A sad-looking clown who's out of a job" to "An alien puppy on a spaceship."

A story is created from the children's responses. If the leader gets stuck, asking "What happens next?" generally gets the story going again. If the balloon bursts on its way around the circle, the crumpled piece is kept, and a new balloon is started. The final story always incorporates the broken piece. It usually works out.

7. NOT ME: HIM!

Number of Players:	6–Unlimited
Age Range:	5–Adult
Preparation:	An inflated balloon
	Live or taped music

All the children stand or sit in a circle. A balloon is passed around to music. As soon as the music stops, whoever is holding the balloon says "NOT ME: HIM/HER!" and tries to toss the balloon to someone else before the music starts again. If the child is successful (the balloon must be accepted when tossed), the game continues. If not, the child that threw the balloon is out.

Whoever is in charge of the music should not look at what is happening, but just vary the time between the stop and start of the music as much as possible. Definitely have a trial round or two for this game.

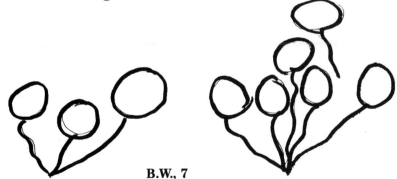

B.W., 7

8. BALLOON FIGHT

Number of Players:	6–Unlimited
Age Range:	7–Adult
Preparation:	Several long-shaped balloons, inflated

The children form a large circle. A volunteer with a long-shaped balloon goes into the center. A challenger comes into the ring, also armed with a long balloon. The two "fighters" face each other, and each one tries to hit the other's balloon with her balloon. The first one to get three "hits" wins, and the next challenger enters the ring. No other contact is allowed. The balloon need not burst, and there is a time limit of one minute before the next competitors start their round. Sometimes, there is no winner, and the round is declared a draw. Some children are afraid of the noise of a balloon bursting, so this is a game best avoided with a very young group, or in a small space. This game is an ideal one to play in a gymnasium or outdoors. Surprisingly, the balloons don't burst as often as you might expect.

9. HOT BALLOON

Number of Players:	6–Unlimited
Age Range:	7–Adult
Preparation:	Several wooden spoons
	A supply of balloons, not blown up
	Two trashbaskets or buckets

Divide the children into teams of equal sizes. If this is not possible, the smaller team may take two turns. Each team is given a supply of balloons and a wooden spoon. At the starting signal, each team must blow up their balloons, and then each team member *in turn* carries his balloon-on-a-spoon to the finish line and deposits it into the bucket. The balloon-on-the-spoon must be carried in one hand and cannot be steadied by the other hand. Keep to a time limit of between five and ten minutes. The team that has the most balloons in the bucket within the time limit wins.

If a balloon is dropped, the team member must return to the starting line. If a balloon bursts, it cannot be replaced.

Any team member can help another in blowing up a balloon.

10. BALLOON IN THE MIDDLE

Number of Players:	6–30
Age Range:	6–Adult
Preparation:	Several inflated round balloons

All the children except one, stand in a large circle. This "odd person out" stands in the middle.

The balloon is tossed at random around the circle, from hand to hand, rolled, bounced, or thrown high. The object of the game is to keep the person in the middle from getting the balloon. If the "odd person" manages to deflect, touch, or intercept the balloon, he changes places with the last person who threw the balloon. A burst balloon is replaced, and that round is repeated.

Stephanie, 9

To Read Aloud:	"Eeyore's Birthday" from *Winnie the Pooh* by A. A. Milne *The Red Balloon* by Albert Lamorisse
Video:	*Winnie the Pooh* ("Pooh and the Honey Bees"—Balloon theme)—Walt Disney
Snack Suggestions:	Pancakes with a variety of toppings or round-shaped sandwiches with banana; cream cheese and date; tuna and mayonnaise fillings. Peanut butter cookies or outsized chocolate chip cookies. Ice cream or chocolate mousse (supermarket variety) served in hollowed-out half oranges.
Invitations:	In the shape of balloons.

Clowns

Basic Motif:	Entertainment
Where:	Indoor/Outdoor

Joanna, 5

"When I get to be an adult, I'll be a clown, I want to be a clown because they are funny and I want to sing songs because I like music—when you sing you cannot be scared."

Lisa, 8

1. CLOWN FACE

Number of Players: 2–20

Age Range: 4–12

Preparation: Makeup sticks: red, silver, gold, white, blue and green

Stars and sparklers

Mirror

3 adults or older children who act as face painters

Table

Cleansing cream

Facial tissues

Soap and water

Paper towels

When guests arrive they go to the table where the makeup artists are waiting for them. The children are given help choosing one of two options. The idea is not to have a full-face makeup, but to set the mood by having just one added feature, both for fun and disguise. Choices may be a red nose, a couple of tears, funny eyebrows, or a star or sparkler across the bridge of the nose. The makeup artists may enjoy creating a heart or a butterfly, but anything more ambitious will cause a very restless lineup.

Meena, 10

2. WHAT KIND OF CLOWN?

Number of Players:	4–20
Age Range:	4–12
Preparation:	None

All the children sit in a circle, and are asked to think about the kind of clown they want to be. The feature they have painted on will help them to make a choice: Sad, silly, happy, stupid, angry, funny or even tired of being a clown.

Then the first child says something like, "I'm Jane and I'm ——," and makes an appropriate face to go with "happy." The other children guess what the face represents. Everyone gets a turn.

3. I'M PLAYING THE BANJO

Number of Players:	4–30
Age Range:	5–Adult
Preparation:	A hat (one with a brim, such as a bowler, is particularly suitable)

Everyone sits in a circle, and the leader starts the game by explaining that clowns use everyday things in out of the ordinary ways. He demonstrates this by treating the hat as if it were something else: a banjo, a steering wheel, or a soup plate. One or two examples are sufficient to inspire the children, and often each one will have several ideas to share. The bowler hat is passed around the circle with everyone taking turns.

A chair can be used in a similar game: the chair is placed in the middle of the circle, and the children are asked to imagine how a clown might use the chair in his act—in a new way. Some examples: as a wheelbarrow, or turned upside down to make a racing car.

4. GRAB THE CLOWN'S HAT

Number of Players: 4–Unlimited

Age Range: 6–Adult

Preparation: Two hats

Two volunteers (Clowns) are each given a hat to wear. The hats should be on the large side. The children stand just far enough apart so that by stretching a little they can touch each other. The object of the game is to grab the other Clown's hat. The rules are these: Clowns must not move their feet from the spot they are standing on. Bodies may stretch, circle, sway, or twist in any direction. If, for instance, Clown #1 is about to snatch the other Clown's hat, Clown #2 might sway, or crouch down out of reach. Talking, shouting, singing, and teasing are allowed—anything that will distract the Clowns' attention. There is a 30-second time limit for hat-grabbing. The first Clown to grab, or pull off the other Clown's hat is the winner, and remains to challenge the next contestant.

5. BOZO

Number of Players: 4–20

Age Range: 6–Adult

Preparation: A chair

Bozo's chair is placed facing the group. A child sits on the chair. To any questions that are put to him, he must reply "BOZO." The players need to keep the questions coming fast, leaving Bozo just enough time to answer each one. For example: "What's your name?" "BOZO." "Where do you live?" "BOZO." "How old are you?" "BOZO." What did you have for dinner?" "BOZO."

If Bozo smiles, laughs, or uses any other word than BOZO,

he is out, and another child takes his place. Allow a 30-second time limit for each contestant.

6. BALL IN THE BOOT

Number of Players:	2–Unlimited
Age Range:	5–Adult
Preparation:	Two large water or work boots
	Two small rubber balls
	A pencil and paper to keep score

This game may be played individually, with each person competing against every other competitor, or it may be played in teams, as follows:

The boots are set up parallel to each other but at least four feet apart. The teams line up behind a starting line between four and five feet away from the boots. Each team member has three chances to throw a ball—or bounce it *once*—into the boot. The leader needs to keep score. Two points are awarded if the ball stays in the boot, one point if it lands in the boot, but bounces out again. The team with the highest score wins.

This is a good outdoor game. Indoors, remove the precious ornaments.

Reann, 8

7. WHERE'S MY SHIRT?

Number of Players: 6–30

Age Range: 5–Adult

Preparation: Old shirts, preferably in a larger size than needed, one for each CLOWN. Turn the shirts inside out and toss them in an untidy jumble on the floor. If there are many players, divide the shirts into two piles.

Divide the competitors into teams of between three to eight Clowns. Then line up the Clowns in order of height, with the smallest in the front. On the words "Find your shirts," the first team members in line run up to the pile, grab a shirt, and put it on. The shirt must be worn correctly, right side out, with all

Andrea, 9

the buttons fastened, before the next team member may start. The first team to be fully dressed, buttoned up, and standing in the same order as at the start of the game, wins.

In a variation of this game, the Clowns take off their own shirts, coats or jackets, and turn them inside out, then the host jumbles them in a pile. In this version of the game, of course, the Clowns must find their own clothing.

8. CLOWN GRAB

Number of Players:	2–Unlimited
Age Range:	4–12
Preparation:	A pail, large saucepan, or basin
	A variety of candies, jellybeans, raisins, nuts, and dried fruits
	or
	Small plastic animals, jacks, marbles, erasers, pennies or collectable items
	A pair of large adult-size clean working gloves (New cotton garden gloves are ideal.)

Peanuts, candies, dried fruits, marbles or pennies are put into a pail. Each Clown (player) in turn puts on the adult-size work gloves. Using the non-preferred hand (a right-handed child would use the left hand), the child gets one turn to pick up a handful of the items in the pail and transfer them to the other hand. If nothing is dropped, the Clown keeps the handful.

In a variation of this game, the Clowns may keep what *remains* in the hand.

This game can get fairly expensive: An alternative method is to *count* the items that each child has managed to grab. Then the child who holds onto the most items wins.

9. DRAW A CLOWN

Number of Players:	4–30
Age Range:	4–12
Preparation:	Live or taped music
	Crayons or felt markers
	Big sheets of paper

Children sit in groups around large sheets of paper, four to a sheet is about right.

Each child is given a colored marker and told to draw a clown—not four different clowns—but all must cooperate to draw *one*, when the music starts playing.

Michael, 10

As soon as the music stops, all drawing must cease. Anyone caught with a marker touching the paper is out. When someone is called "out," it penalizes the whole group, which is given a clean sheet of paper and must start again from scratch, even if their drawing is almost done. This continues until one group calls out "finished." That group is declared the winner.

This game is more difficult than it sounds, because the picture must be filled in. The stop and start of the music should be quick. This game certainly taxes the spirit of artistic cooperation.

10. BUBBLE RACE

Number of Players:	4–20
Age Range:	5–12
Preparation:	Three commercial containers of bubble mixture and wands
	A long piece of ribbon or string
	Paper towels to dry off the contestants
	Paper and pencil for scoring

The ribbon is tied across the room, fastened to the backs of chairs. Children (Clowns) take turns kneeling down (they may stand if they prefer) three or four feet away from the ribbon. Each Clown has three turns for blowing bubbles across the "line" intact. The leader counts the number of bubbles and keeps score.

A "battle" of bubbles is a variation: The children are divided into two teams, and they take up positions on either side of the "battle line" (ribbon). Team members take turns trying to cross a bubble into the "enemy" camp. The leader keeps score as to which is the winning team.

11. CLOWN ACTS

Number of Players:	4–30
Age Range:	6–Adult
Preparation:	A lunch bag per guest
	Each bag contains 4 or 5 simple items, but they may all be different—for instance, a spoon, a rubber band, a toothbrush, an alarm clock, a balloon, an egg timer, a paper hat or a clothes peg

Each guest is given a bag with a few items, and is told that clowns look at ordinary things from an unusual point of view.

Nicole, 6

It's as if they don't know what the "normal" or practical uses are of, say, a toothbrush. That's what makes their acts funny. A balloon might become a clown's dog, or baby, or his act might be about a balloon that doesn't want to be blown up.

The children are given a few minutes to explore the contents of the bags in this light. Then they decide whether to do a solo act or team up with another CLOWN. They work out their acts and perform them for the rest of the group. There is heaps of applause—however short, or "unfinished" the act is.

12. CLOWN BAND

Number of Players:	4–20
Age Range:	3–Adult
Preparation:	The invitations you sent suggested that guests bring a musical instrument, but it's still wise to have a variety of simple, homemade instruments, in addition to kazoos, slide whistles and bells. You can also use rice in a can, beans in a jar, coins in a round cheese box, a cookie tin and wooden spoon, a set of plastic spoons, pebbles in a coffee can, a saucepan with a marble in it, and so on.

Form groups of five or six children. Each member chooses a sound instrument and the "orchestra" is given ten minutes time to practice a tune such as "Yankee Doodle Dandy" or "Three Blind Mice," before performing it for the rest of the group.

This is always a wildly successful end to the party—especially for the 3–10-year-olds.

To Read Aloud:	*Curious George Goes to the Circus* by Margaret Rey *Morgan the Magnificent* by Ian Wallace Or, for very young children *The Toy Circus* by Jan Wahl
Video:	*Dumbo*—Walt Disney
Snack Suggestions:	Spaghetti and meatballs. Chicken chow mein and rice, with eggrolls. Chocolate fondu and fruit for dipping: banana, apple, grapes and strawberries. Chocolate fudge cake.
Invitations:	A simple drawing of a happy or sad clown face wearing a hat. Ask children to come in costume, and to bring a musical instrument or sound maker.

Jennifer, 7

Wild West

Basic Motif: Cowboys and Rodeos
Where: Outdoors, or in a large hall or gymnasium

Michael, 10

*"I see by your outfit that you are a cow-
boy..."*

Anon, "The Streets of Laredo"

1. GAMBLING CASINO

Number of Players: 4–Unlimited (Three adults/helpers are recommended for numbers over 25.)

Age Range: 6–Adult

Preparation: A table covered with a tablecloth of large squares, or white paper designed with empty and filled-in squares

Three plastic tokens or coins for each guest

Prizes of balloons or treats

A piece of checkered cloth or paper, weighed down at each corner, acts as the gaming table. An adult performs the role of croupier. As children arrive, they are each given three tokens or coins with which to gamble. The child (gambler) rolls a coin and if it lands in a square without touching the lines, gets to keep the token and is given an additional one. Coins may be kept at the end of the game or exchanged at the "bank" for balloons or treats. This game should last long enough for every child to have three tosses.

This is a good game to play while guests are arriving, especially if a large number are expected, because anyone can join in at any time. It is an excellent icebreaker.

2. ONE-LEGGED TAG

Number of Players: 6–Unlimited

Age Range: 5–12

Preparation: None

The playing area should be the size of a large room. Designate one area—not too far away—as "safe."

Everyone in this game may only use one leg. The Tagger stands in the center of the room on one leg, waiting to catch the rest of the players, who must try to hop past the Tagger to the "safe place" without being caught. If they are touched, they must join the Tagger. Last one to be caught becomes "It."

3. JAIL TIME

Number of Players:	4–30
Age Range:	5–12
Preparation:	One large Sheriff's badge made up of aluminum foil pasted on a star-shaped card

The child selected as the Sheriff puts on the badge and wanders around the playing space, while being shadowed by the other children (Cattle Rustlers). They call out at intervals, "Got the time, Sheriff?" Then the Sheriff turns around and gives whatever time of day she pleases. All the Cattle Rustlers must freeze the instant she turns and speaks. If she sees anyone move, he is out. When the Sheriff answers "Jail Time," all the Cattle Rustlers run away. If the Sheriff is able to tag them, they go to jail, and are out of the game. The last Cattle Rustler left becomes the new Sheriff.

Everett, 9

4. HORSESHOE TOSS

Number of Players: 4–30

Age Range: 6–Adult

Preparation: A thick piece of wood or dowelling

Jar rings, for horseshoes

Small prizes

Push a stick into a patch of earth. If you're playing this game indoors, use a candle in a holder or a pencil pushed into clay.

Set up a starting line three or four feet away. Competitors line up behind this line in turn to toss rings. Each competitor has three rings. A hat trick (three rings over the obstacles) wins a prize. Very young competitors (9 and under) are given their own starting line at a distance of two feet, and may win with two successful tosses. If the numbers are so large as to cause long waits, two groups may play simultaneously using two sets of sticks and rings.

5. RODEO

Number of Players: 4–30

Age Range: 6–14

Preparation: 2 sets of newspapers rolled up tightly, and fastened with masking tape

The players form a large circle. A timekeeper/observer is inside the ring with two contestants (riders). The Riders each hold a rolled-up newspaper. Each Rider selects a horse from the circle, sits on his shoulders "piggy back style" and faces his opponent on his "horse." The object of the game is for each Rider to knock the newspaper roll out of his opponent's hand. Only the newspaper may be hit, or the Rider is disqualified.

This rule is strictly applied. Maximum time for each round is one minute.

Lots of applause and cheering for their "champion" comes from the circle.

Lemonade is suggested for all four competitors after each battle.

6. WHEELBARROW RACE

Number of Players:	6–30
Age Range:	6–14
Preparation:	None

Two teams are formed, and set a start and finish line for this relay race. One child from each team is the wheelbarrow and walks on his hands; the next person in line holds him by the ankles or legs, wheelbarrow style. As soon as the pair reach the finish line, they change roles and return to the next pair who are waiting to start. If anyone falls, the pair must return to the starting line; if there are two falls, they are disqualified.

It's a good idea to let the children have a practice round or two.

7. WILD PONY

Number of Players:	8–30
Age Range:	5–10
Preparation:	None

A home base is established a short distance away from a circle, formed by all the players. One child, the captive Wild Pony, stands in the middle of the circle. He wants to escape. His captors create a fence by holding onto each others' hands or wrists. If the fence breaks, the Pony may escape. The Pony may also try to push through a weak link in the fenced circle, or try to jump or crawl under. When the Pony gets out, he must reach "Home" before being recaptured.

A new Pony is chosen after the Wild Pony gets home safely. If the Pony doesn't reach home safely within the time limit, his compensation is to choose the next competitor. Set a time limit of a couple of minutes for each round.

Nicole, 6

8. CATTLE RUSTLING

Number of Players:	6–30
Age Range:	6–14
Preparation:	Different colored bandanas (or ribbon for cattle) to denote cowboys and cattle
	Lone Ranger-type half-masks for rustlers
	Score pad and pencil

Divide the children into three groups:

Cowboys (wearing cotton bandanas around their necks that will do double duty as blindfolds)

Cattle (wearing another color of scarf or ribbon) and

Rustlers (wearing half-masks)

Each group starts the game in its own area. The Cowboys sleep (blindfolded) next to the Cattle, who crouch on all fours in the corral. The Rustlers' base is a distance apart from the other groups, on the other side of the cowboys, so it is necessary to pass them to get to the Cattle. The Rustlers' objective is to lead the Cattle to their own base. The Cattle must walk as quietly as possible, on all fours. If the Cowboys hear anything, they may get up and point. If they are clearly seen to point at a Rustler, then he/she is out. If one of the Cattle is being pointed at, it must return to the corral.

The game may be played three times, so the children can have a turn playing each role. The leader keeps track of the most successful Cowboys/Rustlers, and sets a short time limit for each attempt—not more than two minutes, usually—from the time the Cowboys go to sleep.

9. OBSTACLE RACE

Number of Players: 6–30
                          (1 adult per 8 children required)

Age Range: 6–14

Preparation: This is a guide only. Accommodate the obstacle course to the age and stamina of the group.

1. A plank placed across two chairs (leader should make sure the obstacle is steady) for balancing on, crawling across or under.

2. A mattress to crawl under.

3. A rope to jump over.

4. A potato that must be carried on a spoon up a stepladder and down again without being dropped.

5. Blowing up a balloon and tying a knot in it.

6. Blowing bubbles through a straw—the bubbles must float across a rope.

7. A broomstick is held, and contestants go under the stick, touching only their feet to the ground and not using their hands at all.

8. Stacking pieces of firewood in a certain way so they don't fall.

9. Walking on a path of stones, or along a line, with a book balanced on one's head.

10. Running a short distance carrying a mug of water, without spilling a drop.

11. Skipping with a skipping rope around a pre-designated area without stopping.

12. Throwing a lasso around a fencepost or branch from a given distance.

This game may be played individually, in pairs, or in teams. It is important that each activity be tested by the adults in charge. Ideally, children can help to set up and test the safety of the course, which can be designed to fit whatever environment is selected. A timekeeper keeps scores and times to decide the winners.

End with songs or stories around a fire.

To Read Aloud:	Books such as: *Cowboy Small* by Lois Lenski *When I Was Young in the Mountains* by Cynthia Rylant
Video:	*Big Red*—Walt Disney *Across the Great Divide*—Walt Disney
Snack Suggestions:	Hot dogs, hamburgers, homemade lemonade. Peanut butter cookies. Apples and fruit in season. Marshmallows for roasting.
Invitations:	A piece of string glued onto cardboard in the shape of a lasso. Invitations specify appropriate clothing and sneakers.

Saucepans and Sounds (Mainly Pre-School)

Basic Motif: Sounds	Where: Indoors

Tyler, 4½

ME: *Why have you got your feet on the table, Matthew?*
MATTHEW: *There are dragons on the carpet.*

Matthew, 2½

1. QUICK PUPPETS

Number of Players:	2–18
Age Range:	3–10
Preparation:	Newsprint to cover table or floor space
	Paper cups
	Simple craft materials: Foam rubber bits, colored construction paper, corks, scraps of fabric
	Scissors (child size—one between two)
	Felt markers or crayons
	Glue sticks
	(One adult per 6 children required.)

Set out the craft materials in shoe boxes, so that the children can see at a glance the array of choices. Too many ideas are confusing for this age range, so I limit the variety to five or six items. Shoe boxes are ideal for putting the crafts away, before the active games start.

Each child is given a paper cup. They fit beautifully over small hands, and are very easy to decorate, and turn into people, animals or fantasy creatures.

When the children finish making their cups into puppets, they sit in a circle and introduce themselves and their puppet by name. "I'm Sarah—this is a rabbit." The group may agree to make the sounds for the puppets, especially if they are familiar ones. Puppets are an excellent introduction for all guests, and something of a security, for the child attending a first party. They may be taken home at the end of the party.

Treena, 9

2. THE MAGIC DRUM

Number of Players: 5–Unlimited

Age Range: 4–9

Preparation: A chair

A drum and striker. If not available, an upturned saucepan and wooden spoon make an excellent alternative.

The drummer sits on the chair, and drums softly, loudly, fast or slow—the more variety the better. All the children move around in time to the drum sounds. As soon as the drum stops, the children freeze. For young children a good explanation of the word "freeze" is: "Stand as still as a stone." Anyone who moves after the drum stops or before it starts again is out. The last child remaining becomes the new drummer. Play several times, after a trial round.

3. GUESS THE NOISE

Number of Players: 2–Unlimited

Age Range: 4–12

Preparation: None

Children cover their eyes, or sit facing the wall, so they cannot see the leader. A simple noise is made, such as tapping a window or a table, moving a chair, or stamping on the floor three times. The first child to identify the sound correctly becomes the next sound maker. Children are very good at this. A "stretch" is for the leader to make a sequence of three sounds—for example, a clap, a whistle and a hum—and ask the children to identify them in the correct order.

4. WHERE ARE WE?

Number of Players:	6–30
Age Range:	4–10
Preparation:	None

Children sit in a circle. The leader starts off the explanation for this game by asking "What kinds of sounds do you hear when you go to the park? Or to the pet shop?" When the children answer, they are told to make those sounds.

Then a volunteer leaves the room while the group decides on a place it will be in. In a few minutes the child returns and has to guess what the place is. If it is a street, the children would be making the sounds of honking cars and trucks, bicycle bells ringing, or brakes squealing. At the zoo, they would make the sounds of different animals, of people exclaiming, and perhaps the zookeeper calling "Feeding time."

Make sure that each child knows what sound to make (of course, each chooses his own), and that everyone waits for the signal to start. When the volunteer is called back in, she stands in the middle of the circle and everyone makes the noises agreed upon. The volunteer gets three guesses. If her first guess is incorrect, encourage the group to make movements to go with the sounds.

5. HUMMING BALL

Number of Players:	4–Unlimited
Age Range:	4–12
Preparation:	A small, brightly colored ball

A volunteer leaves the room and while he is gone, a small ball is hidden. When the child returns, he is told to find the ball. He will know by the humming sounds made by the others in the room when he is nearing the hiding place.

The closer the volunteer gets to the ball the louder the humming will be. When the humming becomes very soft, or when it disappears completely, the ball is very far away. If the children become tired—and humming can become a strain—substitute clapping. It's a good idea to have a practice round.

6. BARK, DOGGY, BARK!

Number of Players:	5–20
Age Range:	4–8
Preparation:	A blindfold

Everyone sits in a circle and is asked to listen very carefully to the voices of the people in the group, because the next game is about guessing who the voice belongs to without looking.

Each child is told to say his or her first name and then to bark like a puppy.

Now one volunteer stands in the middle of the circle, blindfolded, and is turned around once or twice. The child in the middle points or touches another child and says "Bark, doggy, bark!" If she can identify the owner of the "bark," the children change places, and the game starts again.

7. CATCH ME IF YOU CAN

Number of Players:	5–20
Age Range:	3–8
Preparation:	None

Teach the players this song—to the tune of "Ring Around the Rosy."

"Becky's over the water
Becky's over the sea
Becky caught a big fish
But she can't catch me!"

The children form a circle. One child stands in the middle while the others hold hands and move around, always substituting the name of the child in the middle, for "Becky." If it's a boy, of course, they'll say "He can't catch me!" When they get to the final "me," everyone crouches on the floor as fast as possible, while "Becky" tries to tag someone. If she manages to touch anyone before that child is stooping safely on the floor, they change places.

8. HUNT THE SAUCEPAN

Number of Players:	5–20
Age Range:	3–10
Preparation:	A blindfold
	A large saucepan and lid
	A plastic or wooden spoon
	A small attractively gift-wrapped present for each child

This game requires a large space, cleared of precious ornaments. The children are warned to keep well out of the way of the "searching spoon."

One child is blindfolded, handed the spoon and told to find the saucepan, which has a gift in it. The only way to find the saucepan is to crawl around on the floor tapping with the spoon. The other children can shout instructions, such as, "Keep going," or "Wrong way!" Once the child taps the saucepan, the blindfold and lid are removed, and the present unwrapped and kept. Everyone watches each gift being unwrapped. Then the saucepan is hidden in a different spot for the next player.

Ask the children to make noise while the saucepan is being hidden, if you want to make the game more difficult. The competitors get very good at listening for the sound of the lid covering "their gift"!

An important safety measure: It's a good idea to set space limits. For example, establish the fact that the saucepan is on the carpet—or on the part that is *not* carpeted.

Like "Poison Candy" (on page 20) this game has been a favorite in our family for many years. The players never seem to mind the long wait for their turn.

To Read Aloud:	*Mortimer* by Robert Munsch *The Little Old Lady Who Was Not Afraid of Anything* by Linda Williams *What's That Noise?* by Michele Lemieux
Video:	*Paddington Bear* *Winnie the Pooh and Friends*—Walt Disney
Snack Suggestions:	Fruit jello made in empty yogurt containers. Carrot, apple and cheese slices. Peanut butter, banana and jam sandwiches, cut in fingers. Cupcakes decorated with sprinkles, bits or candies. Miniature chocolate eclairs.
Invitations:	With a drum and a striker, or any musical instrument, and a happy face.

The Great Outdoors

Randy, 8

"I like camping out, nature and wilderness. I want to find out what it's like being all alone."

Jason, 10

1. PICK A NAME

Number of Players: 6–30

Age Range: 6–Unlimited

Preparation: Blank stickers on name tags, one per guest

Several felt pens

An assortment of old shirts in large sizes

When the guests arrive, if they are not already wearing camping gear, as specified on the invitations, they may borrow one of the old shirts you have on hand.

Each arrival is asked to choose an "alias," or a name that would suit a new lifestyle in the great outdoors. You might have a suggested list of names ready for younger children such as Sunshine, Boots, Sam Sneakers, Millie Mud.

Of course any name will do.

2. MEMORIES

Number of Players: 6–30

Age Range: 6–Adult

Preparation: A can of food with a bright label such as is found on a can of beans

To set the mood, pass around a can of food. The guests will hold the can while introducing themselves by their new names and adding their favorite food, one that they might eat on a campout. For example: "I'm Bill Branch, I like beans." This information is repeated by the next child in the circle, and one more name and food item is added: "I'm Bill Branch, I like beans," and "I'm Charlie and I like cookies," and so on around the circle.

This memory game sets the atmosphere for the theme. You can vary it by using place names instead of food. Places can be anywhere in the world, and the game works in the same way. For instance: "I'm Betty and I walked to the Pacific Ocean." For older children who want even more of a challenge, the food or place name may start with the same letter as the chosen name: "I'm Annie, and I walked to Antarctica."

3. WET FEET

Number of Players:	6–30
Age Range:	6–Adult
Preparation:	Some lively music on radio or tape. Live music such as harmonica or kazoo is fun.
	Sheets of newspaper, at least one dozen
	A large space cleared of as much furniture as possible is essential for this game.

Spread sheets of newspaper at random on the ground, but leaving enough space so that the children (Campers) can move *around* them. When the music plays, the Campers move in rhythm around the newspapers—but do not step on them—until the music stops. Then the papers are designated as DRY GROUND and all the Campers rush onto them to keep "their feet dry."

As many people as possible crowd onto the papers; anyone not on "dry ground" within a slow count of five after the music stops, is out. No part of anyone's body may be off the paper. After each round, as children are eliminated, sheets of paper are removed, until finally only one sheet is left. The all-time record is 15 children on one sheet of newspaper. For maximum excitement, vary the length of time the music plays.

4. PASS THE BOOT

Number of Players:	6–30
Age Range:	6–Adult
Preparation:	An old boot, sneaker or shoe
	Live or taped music

Everyone (the Campers) stands in a circle, with sufficient room to stretch. The boot is very old and worn, and no one wants to hold it. The Campers pass the boot around the circle, and when the music stops, whoever is holding the boot is out. Change the stop and the start of the music quickly. The game continues until only one Camper is left—the winner.

5. SHOE SCRAMBLE

Number of Players:	8–30
Age Range:	6–Adult
Preparation:	None

Divide the children into teams (ten is the maximum size for a team). They take off their left shoes. These shoes are put in a heap in the middle of the floor and thoroughly mixed up by the leader. Each team member is numbered from one to ten (or however many numbers are in each team). When the leader calls out a number—6, for example—all the sixes from the teams retrieve their shoes, put them on, tie the laces, and sit down. The next number, say 3, is called within a slow count of five. However, the #3 team member is not allowed to come forward until the #2 team member has located her shoe, put it on and is sitting down. This means at any one time three or four different numbers are all at different stages of finding, wearing, and tying up shoes. It also ensures that a manageable number of children are at the shoe pile, at any one time.

The first team correctly shod, and sitting down wins.

You can also play this game using shirts instead of shoes, and insist all shirts are buttoned up! (See page 92.). Team members are permitted to help lace up shoes, or button shirts. You can make the game even more difficult by turning shirt sleeves inside out, and requiring that they be turned the right way before being put on.

6. GUESS HOW MANY

Number of Players:	2–Unlimited
Age Range:	6–Adult
Preparation:	A jar, ice bucket, or any other container or glass bottle filled with small items: pennies, nickels, jelly beans, marbles, tacks, shells, or stones
	A paper and pencil for each guest
	A small prize

Display the jar of small objects for about 30 seconds. Then contestants write their names on the paper along with their estimate of the number of objects they think the jar holds. The items are publicly counted and the guess that is closest to the correct number wins the prize.

Children love the tension of the public count; there need not be a huge number of items. It's surprising how difficult it is to guess that there are 108 M&M's in a yogurt container.

Everett, 9

7. THE ARTFUL DODGER

Number of Players:	6–Unlimited
Age Range:	6–Adult
Preparation:	An assortment of bandanas, dust rags, handkerchiefs, scarves or ties—one for each player. Contestants will need a belt or pocket.

There's no telling who you'll run into on your travels cross-country. This game, inspired by the Dickens novel *Oliver Twist*, puts you in touch with the criminal element—and it's *you*! It is excellent for calming a noisy, energetic group because it needs great concentration to make it work.

One person is chosen to be the Sheriff. Everyone else tucks a bandana or scarf into the back of a belt, through a belt loop, or into a pocket. The cloth must protrude so that it can be seen. Set a time limit of three or four minutes. The object of the game is for every competitor to "steal" as many items as possible in the time allotted, without being caught red-handed by the Sheriff. The rules are: Keep moving, at any speed and in any direction. If the Sheriff catches a Camper in the act, holding the stolen goods, the Camper is out. Every Camper is pitted against everyone else, *and* against the Sheriff. Whoever has the most stolen goods at the end of three minutes is the winner. Plan several rounds.

Danielle, 10

8. BROWN BAG

Number of Players:	2–Unlimited
Age Range:	6–Adult
Preparation:	15 ordinary objects of the kind that a camper might need on a long trip, such as razor (not electric), a sweat band, a dollar bill, a box of matches, a piece of chalk, a deck of cards, a candle stub, a pair of socks, soap, needle and thread, a can opener, a spoon, a knife and fork, a water bottle, a scarf, comb, a newspaper
	A brown paper bag
	A cloth
	Pencil and paper
	Small prizes

Keep the objects in the brown paper bag until you're ready to play the game. Then empty the contents of the bag. Give the children one minute to memorize all the items. Now cover all the objects. The campers team up with one or two partners and list as many of the items as they can. There is a prize for the first correct solution—or the most correct one. Then ask them to turn around while one item is removed. Ten seconds are allowed for determining which object is missing, before the object is returned.

Treena, 9

9. SHAKE THE HAT

Number of Players: 2–Unlimited

Age Range: 7–Adult

Preparation: A hat and a pair of dice

Pencil and paper for scoring

A small prize

Two of everything, if the game is played in two groups

If you're playing with large numbers of children, you can set up this game with two groups. Have two adults on hand—one to put down the scores for each group.

Put the dice into the hat. The hat is shaken by each competing camper, and then turned upside down onto a flat surface. Each competitor has three rolls of the dice. The adult adds up the scores and marks them down. The Camper with the highest score in each group wins the prize.

Everett, 9

122

10. SCAVENGER HUNT

Number of Players:	4–Unlimited
Age Range:	7–Adult
Preparation:	A pencil and notebook for each team
	A list for each team
	A simple map for each team (The map marks 4 or 5 different locations at which the teams have to check in after completing specific tasks, such as counting windows, etc. For example: THE OLD TREE STUMP, THE HOLLOW LOG, THE ROUND POND, THE SHED, THE BRICK PILE, etc.)
	5 adults—one at each location

Each member of the winning team gets a prize.

Children may work in pairs, threes or larger teams. Each group is given a map, a notebook and pencil and the list of ten to fifteen tasks, questions, and things to find. Each list should be identical but in a different sequence so that children won't be doing everything at the same time. The kind of list will vary in its questions, depending on the location of the party, and the age of the participants.

A sample list might look like this:

FIND something with writing on it, such as a sign, a note or a poster.

DRAW the nearest sign, such as KEEP OFF THE GRASS.

COUNT the numbers of windows in this building. When you finish, check in at THE OLD TREE STUMP.

FIND something red, something to eat, something with the letter "S" on it.

WRITE down two ingredients needed when baking bread, or preparing a meal outdoors.

COLLECT five twigs for starting a campfire. Check in at THE HOLLOW LOG.

COUNT the number of trees on route 2 marked on the map.

It is important to keep the hunt within a prescribed area, with the adults at checkpoints as part of the game. Each child or team gets a checkmark from the adult manning the location. This also works as a *safety* feature. Children must know which areas are part of the hunt and which are out of bounds. All hunts end at a designated "HOME" base. Set a time limit. The scavenger hunt may be held indoors, or as a combination of both indoors/outdoors. It can be as simple or as complicated as time and interest permit.

Gregory, 7

11. CAMPFIRE TIME

Number of Players:	4–Unlimited
Age Range:	6–Adult
Preparation:	None

Each Camper entertains the group around the campfire. The entertainment can be a song, a dance, a funny story, or an imaginary adventure of "When I was on the road yesterday." Tall tales are always popular, and younger children can be given an example such as: "Yesterday I was camping by the river, and a trout jumped straight from the river into my frying pan. That was the best supper I ever ate."

To Read Aloud:	*The Sign of the Beaver* by Elizabeth George Speare *The Courage of Sarah Noble* by Alice Dalgliesh
Video:	*The Wind in the Willows—* Walt Disney
Snack Suggestions:	Pancakes and bacon, hot dogs and beans, or chili and garlic bread. Chocolate cake or muffins. Hot chocolate and marshmallows.
Invitations:	In the shape of a pair of sneakers, or a backpack. Dress up in camping gear.

Age Range Chart and Game Index

	PAGE	4-5	6-7	8-12	12-Adult
Act a Hobby	25			★	★
Animal Masks	63	★	★	★	★
Artful Dodger	120		★	★	★
Ball in the Boot	91	★	★	★	★
Balloon Face	81	★	★	★	
Balloon Fight	84		★	★	★
Balloon in the Middle	85		★	★	★
Balloon Race	80	★	★	★	★
Balloon Story	82	★	★	★	
Bark, Doggy, Bark	112	★	★		
Blow Out the Candle	37		★	★	★
Bobbing for Apples	36	★	★	★	★
Bozo	90		★	★	★
Brown Bag	121		★	★	★
Bubble Race	95	★	★	★	
Campfire Time	125		★	★	★
Carolling	52		★	★	★
Catch Me If You Can	112	+★	★		
Cattle Rustling	105		★	★	★
Circus Seals	80	★	★	★	★
Clown Acts	96		★	★	★
Clown Band	97	+★	★	★	★
Clown Face	88	★	★	★	
Clown Grab	93	★	★	★	
Crime Has Been Committed	15			−★	★
Doughnut Gobble	38		★	★	★
Draw a Clown	94	★	★	★	
Ducks and Ptarmigans	47		★	★	★
Experts	29			−★	★
Fill the Stockings	49		★	★	★
Find the Animal	58	★	★	★	★
Find the Balloon	79	★	★	★	★
Find the Bomb	13		★	★	★
Flashlight Faces	39		★	★	★
Floating Balloons	79	★	★	★	★
Forgotten Card	54	★	★	★	★
Gambling Casino	100		★	★	★
Get Your Apple	39		★	★	★
Ghost Story	41		★	★	★
Grab the Clown's Hat	90		★	★	★
Guess How Many	119		★	★	★
Guess the Noise	110	★	★	★	
Hats, Props, and Costumes	31			★	★

+★: Age 3–5   /★: Upper end of age level   ★/: Lower end of age level
−★: Age 9 Up   ★−: Up to Age 9   ★★−: Up to Age 14

Age Range Chart and Game Index

	PAGE	4-5	6-7	8-12	12-Adult
Heart Mosaic	76	★	★	★	★
Hidden Loot	11		★	★	★
Horseshoe Toss	102		★	★	★
Hot Balloon	84		★	★	★
Humming Ball	111	★	★	★	
Hunt the Deer	60		★	★	★
Hunt the Saucepan	113	+★	★	★	
I Caught a Thief, He Was Doing This ...	16			★	★
I'm Playing the Banjo	89	★	★	★	★
Impossible Hearts	76	★	★	★	★
In the News	27			★	★
I Sent My Love a Valentine	71		★	★	★
Jail Time	101	★	★	★	
Kangaroos Fly	61	★	★		
Let Me Out	41		★	★	★
Lucky Dip	55	★	★	★	★
Magic Drum	110	★	★	★−	
Make a Commercial	30		★	★	★
Make a Mask	34		★	★	★
Marriage Proposal	74		★	★	★
Memories	116		★	★	★
Meow, Kitty, Meow	64	★	★	★	★
Mime Relay Race	26			★	★
Mug Shot	17		★		
Murder Investigation	18			★	★
Musical Candy	49	★	★	★	★
Mystery Code	17			★	★
Not Me: Him!	83	★	★	★	★
Nursery Rhymes	62	★	★	★	★
Obstacle Race	106		★	★	★★
One-Legged Tag	100	★	★	★	
One Word Valentine	71		★	★	★
Pass the Boot	118		★	★	★
Pick a Name	16		★	★	★
Picture Valentine	72		★	★	★
Playfully	28			★	★
Poison Candy	20	★	★	★	★
Prickly Porcupine	65		★	★	★
Puppet Story	66	★	★	★	
Quick Puppets	109	+★	★	★	
Rhyming Spells	43			★	★
Rodeo	102		★	★	★★
Scavenger Hunt	123		★	★	★
Shake the Hat	122		★	★	★

127

Age Range Chart and Game Index

	PAGE	4-5	6-7	8-12	12-Adult
Shoe Scramble	118		★	★	★
Silent Witness	14				
Sit Beside Me, Please	24		★	★	★
Sit on My Knee	70	★	★	★	★
Snake in the Grass	59	★	★	★	
So Many Words	73			★	★
Spin a Story	27			★	★
Steal the Treasure	11		★	★	★
Step on My Heart	69	★	★	★	★
Stolen Money	10		★	★	★
Toy Shop	48	★	★	★	★
Valentine Countdown	69	★	★	★	★
Valentine Mime Relay	75		★	★	★
Wake the Witch	40		★	★	★
Welcome	35		★	★	
Wet Feet	117		★	★	★
What Am I Doing?	23		★	★	★
What Does the Snowman Say? Nothing!	47	★	★	★	★
What Kind of Clown?	89	★	★	★	
What's in the Parcel?	50	★	★	★	★
Wheelbarrow Race	103		★	★	★★-
When I Grow Up ...	24			★	★
Where Are We?	111	★	★	★	
Where's My Shirt?	92	★	★	★	★
Where's My Tail?	64	★	★	★	★
Who Am I?	58	★	★	★	★
Who Are You?	13		★	★	★
Wild Pony	103	★	★	★	
Winter Birds	46	★	★	★	★
Winter Scenes	52		★	★	★
Witch Tag	37		★	★	★
Wrap the Gifts	51		★	★	★

+★: Age 3–5   /★: Upper end of age level   ★/: Lower end of age level
−★: Age 9 Up   ★−: Up to Age 9   ★★−: Up to Age 14